puppetry and eastern shadow puppetry, with their strange forms, ancient rituals, taboos, mystic significance and rich language of gesture and mime.

The 16 color plates and 76 pages of black-and-white illustrations with detailed captions bring to life this magnificent collection of puppets. Among the mechanical figures illustrated are a gymnast performing on a horizontal bar; a clown who simultaneously sings and conducts a braying donkey; trick figures like the peddler who can be transformed instantly into a pig. Also included are surrealistic illusions, magic lanterns, etc.

This book is an attractive introduction to puppetry, full of fascinating details which evoke the feeling of enchantment unique to the wonderful world of puppets.

Günter Böhmer   The Wonderful World of Puppets

Günter Böhmer

THE WONDERFUL WORLD OF
PUPPETS

Translated by Gerald Morice

Based on the Puppet Collection of the City of Munich

Publishers PLAYS, INC. *Boston*

Editorial assistant: Columba Wilhem

Photographs by Dagmar Perls,
Bettina von Waldthausen, Peter Raba,
Bettina Böhmer, Herbert Benn,
Lotte Beyschlag, Erica Zollitsch

*Picture on cover: a prince, Munich. Early
this century. See caption to illustration 29*

Published in Great Britain under the
title, *Puppets*.
First American Edition
published by Plays, Inc. 1971
Library of Congress Catalog
Card Number: 76-107968
Blocks, setting and printing:
F. Bruckmann KG, Munich
Graphische Kunstanstalten.
Printed in Germany.
ISBN: 0-8238-0084-9

Foreword

Puppets cannot be fully effective within the framework of a collection, for their natural setting is not a museum but a theatre, even if it is only a booth thronged by a gaping public on a fairground where once, for all their roughness and simplicity, they reached their historic peak.

Historic puppets, not very many of which have survived, certainly deserve honoured places in museums, but there is a danger that they will be assigned a wrong artistic category if an individual figure is regarded as sculpture and, as a plastic creation, placed on the same level. If, accustomed to take a very broad view of the term 'work of art', one is led to look on puppets as sculptures, the most essential part of their artistic purpose may easily be overlooked or even falsified, for the figures in a puppet theatre acquire life and soul only when they are set in motion with the aid of strings or rods or directly by the puppeteer's hand.

Touchingly lively as their originality may be, and for all their obstinate individuality, in the final analysis all puppets are no more than instruments of the puppeteer. They are subject to his will and the skill of his manipulation. In general they require the human voice or musical accompaniment as well as an extensive apparatus of lights and scenery to display their indefinable appeal to its full extent. In any event, a sensitive puppeteer is always ready to identify himself completely with his puppet, to let himself be inspired by it and to subordinate himself to it.

For these reasons, a virtuoso puppeteer will maintain that it is not he but his puppet who determines the performance.

Off stage all puppets look weak and unsteady. Since that is what they literally are, all sorts of devices are needed to support them and to give

5

them a life-like appearance. A change in its surroundings, however, has little or no effect on a strong figure.

Many puppets, from the caravans of long-vanished travelling theatres, possess such impressive personalities, such archaic powers of expression, that one can term them complete works of art. And, unintentionally, this is what they certainly are. The Asiatic shadow figures, too, have a graphic charm and delicacy which satisfy the highest artistic standards. Yet their makers were merely anonymous craftsmen, who worked on roughly-tanned animal skins with knives and graving tools, using traditional patterns.

Puppets cannot be isolated from other disciplines, to which they are linked in many ways: the fine arts and performing arts, literature and legend, folklore and sociology, and even journalism and contemporary comment.

Nor can they be excluded from the magic twilight of illusion and the unreal, which enables the imagination to transform creations of wood and papier-mâché, fabric and wire, into beings of flesh and blood. The puppet theatre is a masterly art of illusion. Its reality, based on deception and conjuring, collapses like a house of cards if it is moved into a relentless light, or studied in too close or too penetrating a proximity. This is a psychological fact; and so every stage is a certain spatial distance from its audience.

Schiller's well-known verse: *Der Schein soll nie die Wirklichkeit erreichen, und siegt Natur, so muß die Kunst entweichen* (the appearance should never reach reality and if nature wins art must disappear) seems almost to have been specially coined for puppetry. This aversion to the light, almost a professional condition, and a characteristic of the showman's calling in earlier centuries, may well account for the fact that the history of the puppet theatre is still to a large extent obscure.

When puppeteers were vagrants on the highways and did not consider themselves to be artists, the last thing they thought of doing was to write down any biographical details about themselves for their contemporaries or those who would come after. Many excellent operators could not even state the exact date of their births. Popular as the puppet theatre always was in all its regional forms, it was labelled a street entertainment and it found but few chroniclers. That is why its documentation is scarce, and absolutely a matter of chance. It is only recently that research has started seriously to concern itself with the phenomenon of the taste for 'pop' and the trivial and for the 'underground' in art and style.

That there are so few traces, and that they are so vague, is also, of course, to be ascribed to the perishable nature of puppets. They were no more than tools of their trade to the wandering puppeteers, constantly repaired and freshly painted, finally thrown away as rubbish when they had served their purpose. Posterity has been deprived of many important figures through the old custom, on the death of a puppet master, of laying beside him in the grave his prize creations.

Philological evidence confirms that the origins of puppetry lie in the dawn of ancient cultures, in the myths of gods and idol worship.

The terms in use in the Javanese shadow theatre—*wayang* for the theatre, *dalang* for the puppeteer and *kelir* for the screen—are derived from a pre-

6

historic language period. The nightly performances, with figures of perforated and painted buffalo leather, illustrate the ancient legend of Rama.

A religious source is assumed also for the Greek marionettes of clay, wood, wax, ivory and sometimes bronze and ivory, called *agalmata neurospasta* (pictures moved by strings). The literature of antiquity confirms the prevalence of puppetry in the Greek Mediterranean area. Xenophon in his *Symposium* mentions performances by travelling players from Syracuse. Athenaeus in his *Deipnosophists* refers to a puppeteer called Potheinos who, to the annoyance of the Sophists, was allowed to perform in the theatre of Dionysus at Athens, in the place where the plays of Euripides had been given. Plato, Aristotle, Horace and the satirist, Persius Flaccus, indulge in metaphors and similes about the lack of liberty of human beings who are only marionettes in the hands of gods.

Whether the puppets travelled from the ancient world in the baggage of the Roman mercenaries or later in a roundabout way through Moorish Spain to northern Europe, or by both means simultaneously, still awaits more precise clarification by scholars, who only now are directing their attention to this extraordinarily rich field of research.

One finds pictures of puppets in the Middle Ages, in the *Hortus deliciarium* of Abbess Herrad von Landsperg in which, under the designation *Ludus monstrorum*, are shown two puppets controlled by horizontally-held strings (somewhat in the manner of the *marionnettes à la planchette*), and in the illuminated manuscript at the Bodleian Library, Oxford, of the *Roman du bon roi Alexandre* of 1344, in which there are two miniatures of hand-puppet booths.

Evidence becomes more concrete and frequent in the sixteenth century, through the records of the city councils, in which the names of puppeteers seeking permission to perform are entered.

The eighteenth and nineteenth centuries must be regarded as the golden age of European puppetry when, after the ban on Hanswurst from the 'live' stage, it took sole possession of the old popular theatre. In an atmosphere of romantic preoccupation with popular traditions, puppetry—with rough and coarse characters and plays—kept alive a world which had become anachronistic.

Right into our own times puppetry has constantly remained, with all its comic, horrible and sentimental stock personages, a miniature theatre—that is, an imitation of the 'live' theatre and its players. Even the artistic puppet theatre which, through new aims and standards, preserved puppetry from decay has not been able in the course of emancipation to free itself from the official theatre.

Only recently has there been consideration of the possibilities of theatre specifically for puppets. These lie in the full exploitation of illusion and surrealist opportunities which are not available in the actors' theatre. They find in the puppet theatre in particular an adequate expression of our highly technical times, so receptive to experiment. This fruitful self-analysis has already had the effect that in Eastern Europe puppetry, as an independent form of theatre, enjoys the same rights as the 'live' theatre.

7

The survey of forms of puppetry and types of figures presented here is also a cross-section of the resources of the Puppentheatersammlung der Stadt München (Puppet Collection of the City of Munich). No claim for completeness is made for this survey. Nor could this be even if more space were available, since the theme, that of puppetry in all its historic and ethnological forms, has yet to be covered in any collection.

A puppet collection—there are comparable institutions in Moscow, Dresden, Lyons and Detroit—if only by reason of its subject has something special and singular about it, which many other museums do not as a matter of course possess. It is exceptional because of its homely atmosphere and its humanity which contrast with the still prevalent view that a museum is an awe-inspiring place, to be entered on tiptoe.

The sympathetic quality that puppets have of drawing children under their spell, and of appealing in the most uncomplicated manner to the hearts of their audiences, does not make it easy for a puppet museum, which finds itself involuntarily playing on the public's emotions, properly to indicate its significance as a learned institution. In this respect the same tenacious prejudices are manifest, unfortunately, as those which would label puppetry for all time as a children's amusement and a fairground entertainment.

The evolution of the Puppentheatersammlung as a unique, specialized museum, reaching out over Europe, Africa and Asia, having points of contact with and uniting a multiplicity of fields of knowledge, has by no means followed an intentional, precisely prescribed course. There were no comparable examples or models to follow, let alone other points of departure. Instead the Collection grew with organic consistency within an area largely ignored and neglected by research, and its accumulation was pioneer work in this no man's land.

It goes without saying that the museum was created in the knowledge that there was being continued a tradition of the city of Munich, which in 1909 led the world in establishing a permanent marionette theatre.

The start of the Collection goes back to the fateful year 1939 when the outbreak of war brought the preparation of an exhibition of South German puppetry to such a sudden end that a considerable proportion of the assembled exhibits remained in Munich. Under the pressure of clearance orders, many of those who had lent items were glad to be relieved of the worry as to what to do about their puppets and documents.

So the city took into its care a number of fine old stage sets and with skill and good luck saved them from destruction. Other objects handed over at the same time to the Munich Theatre Museum (the Clara-Ziegler-Stiftung) unfortunately perished during the war.

The custody of the puppet material salvaged by the city of Munich during the years of disaster and ruin was the responsibility of a municipal official, Ludwig Krafft. Thoroughly unbureaucratic, he made puppetry the major interest of his life. The bitter knowledge that the indifference of those who came after would have a more disastrous effect than the bombing and the looting on such possessions as the puppeteers might leave behind them aroused in him an almost missionary zeal to rescue as much as possible.

Anonymous nineteenth-century vignette of a harlequin

So to Ludwig Krafft this Collection, which he founded and represented for so many years, owes its growth, expansion and reputation.

This present publication, too, which he left to his successor, has its foundations in his praiseworthy activities.

European Puppets

1 OPIZ, George Emanuel
(born 1776 in Prague; died 1841 in Leipzig)
Kasperltheater.
Gouache. Signed and dated 1805.
27.5 by 38 cm.
In the manner of Boilly's physiognomic studies, the artist, a master of the bourgeois genre, observes the highly-amused spectators of a hand-puppet show. They could be a land owner with his family and servants. The style of the performance bears a certain resemblance to that of the Commedia dell'Arte.

2 HOGARTH, William
(born 1697 in London; died 1764 in London)
Southwark Fair.
Engraving. "Invented Painted & Engraved by W. Hogarth." 1733.
36.2 by 46.7 cm.
Players, prostitutes, pickpockets, men running races for a wager, peep-show (or raree) men, quacks, musicians and puppet showmen take part in the bewildering kaleidoscope of this fair. In the famous *Observations on Hogarth's Satires* by G. C. Lichtenberg (1742—99), in the course of a commentary on Southwark Fair (described by the writer as "the true haunt of the rabble in London") there is a passage about Punch, claiming that he may be seen on a placard in front of one of the booths. "With a companion and a wheelbarrow he [Punch] is moving towards Hell's Mouth [the jaws of destruction]. In the process he engages in combat with a kindred spirit, a Harlequin or Pulcinello, introduced from the Continent. He probably does so with his fists, in British style, for Punch is renowned for his bravery, as he regularly shows by slaying the Devil."

3 BRYARD, H. C.
(born 1812 at Hartford; died 1881 in New York)
Punch-Theatre.
Oil painting on canvas. Signed and dated 1851.
30 by 45.5 cm.
A Punch performer has set up his booth in the street of a little English town. A drummer seeks to attract spectators. A terrifying Punch figure, with a red face, staring eyes and a hump, in a red peaked hat and a doublet, peers out from the stage opening. See *Briefe eines Verstorbenen* (Letters of a Dead Man) by Prince Pückler-Muskau (1830—2) for a description of a typical Punch and Judy show.

4 DURA, Giovanni (First half of the nineteenth century)
Zampognare che fa ballare i burattini.
Coloured lithograph by Gatti and Dura.
Signed G. Dura and dated 1851.
29.3 by 18 cm.
A bagpipe player sets two puppets dancing to the rhythm of his music. An example of *marionnettes à la planchette*.

5 MAGIOTTO, Francesco
(born 1750 in Venice; died 1805 in Venice)

Punch on his travels, by George Cruikshank.
(From "Punch and Judy", edited by John Payne Collier, 1828, from the performance of Signor Piccini, with illustrations by George Cruikshank)

I Burattini/Les Marionnettes.
Engraving. Franc. Magiotto inv. Car. Paroli del. Amad. Gabrieli sculpsit.
22 by 33.5 cm.
Cicerone e Demostene non vanta
Tanta facondia quanta Pulcinella,
Quando parla costui ciascuno incanta
C fa doler dal rider le mascella.
(Cicero and Demosthenes cannot boast such a verbal fluency as Pulcinella; for, when he speaks, he so bewitches every one that their cheeks ache from laughing.)
On a street corner a blind violinist plays for a performance by a Venetian puppeteer, who has emerged from the side of his booth to argue with his Pulcinella.

6 LANTÉ, Louis Marie (born 1789)
Paris, Bonne d'Enfant.
Coloured engraving. Signed Lanté del Gatine sculpt.
33.7 by 23.4 cm.
A Parisian nursemaid with a harlequin marionette.

7 GRANDVILLE, Jacques Isidor
(born 1803 at Nancy; died 1847 at Vauve, near Paris)
"Je l'aurai! tu ne l'auras pas
je l'aurai! tu ne l'auras pas
bouhuu . . . !"

Coloured lithograph by Delaporte. Chez Aubert, Paris.
La Caricature; No. 69.
19 by 15.2 cm.
Political caricature of Louis Philippe. Marianne threatens to kill him with the aid of an iron fist.

8 GAVARNI, Paul
(born 1804 in Paris; died 1866 at Auteuil)
Illusionist.
Pen and ink sketch. Signed Gavarni.
24.5 by 19.2 cm.
A caricature by Gavarni of an unidentified conjurer and illusionist, one of his contemporaries — it could be the photographer, aeronaut and all-round artist, Nadar. The picture also shows Polichinelle, who was more and more displaced by Guignol in the course of the nineteenth century.

9 DAUMIER, Honoré
(born 1808, or possibly 1810, at Marseilles; died 1879 at Valmondois)
Les Principaux Personnages de la Comédie qui se joue en ce moment aux Champs-Elysées.
Lithograph from *La Caricature.* Chez Aubert, Paris.
24.5 by 35 cm.
Topical satire on a dispute between politicians.

10 COYPEL, Charles Antoine
(born 1699 in Paris, where he died in 1752)
Don Quixote attacking a marionette theatre.
Engraving. Signed Car. Coypel pinx, B. Picart sculp.
22 by 16 cm.
("Don Quixote, believing the marionettes to be Moors, thinks, in fighting them, that he is aiding two fugitive Amans.")
The theatre is reduced to ruins under the blows from Don Quixote's sword. The terrified puppeteer tries to oppose "the Knight with the doleful countenance".

11 TESCHNER, Richard
(born 1879 at Karlsbad; died 1948 in Vienna)
Marionettedrama.
Oil painting on canvas. Signed and dated 1904.
88.5 by 80.5 cm.
A fairy-tale king in an ermine robe stabs the lover of the Princess with his sword. In her hands the Princess holds her beloved's heart. At the feet of the melancholy king gesticulates a sprite-like red Kasperl — a real Bohemian Kasparek, such as Teschner would have met in the puppet theatre when he established himself in Prague in 1902.
Richard Teschner, painter and illustrator in the late period of the "Jugendstil", had a rod-puppet theatre of great aesthetic quality. In 1931 this was given the name Figurenspiegel ("Figure Mirror") and it achieved a reputation far beyond Vienna.

12 WALDMÜLLER, Ferdinand Georg
(born 1793 in Vienna; died 1865 at Helmstreitmühle, near Vienna)
Kinderlust.
Lithograph by Weixelgartner after a painting by Waldmüller (1850).
41.8 by 54.3 cm.
In a draughty barn a peep-show man exhibits his pictures to a crowd of country people, consisting mostly of children.

13 THE MONOGRAMMATIST "FS"
(Anonymous)
Potato Theatre.

Lithograph on a plate.
Signed with an interwoven FS.
34 by 30 cm.
An artist is rehearsing his hand puppets by candlelight. As figures, he is using head-shaped potatoes, which he has carved with a knife and placed on his forefingers. Two visitors, unobserved by him, amuse themselves by watching through the half-opened door, which may later serve as a stage.
The potato theatre is a simplified form of hand puppetry, in which a handkerchief, placed over the hand, simulates the dress, and the thumb and middle fingers the two arms.

14 SHOWMAN'S POSTER
Schichtls Fantoches Fantastiques.
Chromolithograph. Signed C. Schichtl, and dated 1910.
150 by 108 cm.
Franz Xaver Schichtl (born 1849 in Munich; died 1925 in Hanover) was the son of J. E. Ignaz Schichtl, "Mechanikus und Kabinettbesitzer" (mechanician and Ambulant Speciality proprietor) and of the daughter of the puppeteer Georg Michael Deppert. He became world-famous through his tours of many countries with his illusionistic trick figures. His son, Xaver (born 1888), had fantastic ideas equal to those of his father. This poster told the world of the sensational attractions of the widespread Schichtl family of showmen.

15 THEATRE CURTAIN (stage front curtain)
Painted by Joseph Palta. About 1930.
From Kuno Ossberger's marionette theatre, Munich.
On canvas.
175 by 108 cm.
Kasperl is shown as Apollo in a chariot drawn by white horses and surrounded by the Nine Muses. A silhouette of Munich appears on the horizon, in the background.
Kasperl wears peasant dress of the Lungau district of Salzburg consisting of a red jacket, yellow trousers and a peaked hat, and dated about 1800.

48   Inhabitants of Hades
19th century Austrian marionettes
(colour plate I)

50 Clown
Early 19th century English marionette
(colour plate II)

Hand Puppets

The hand puppet is the simplest form of puppet, although it demands aptitude, effort and capacity for psychological understanding to transform a figure, consisting merely of a head, the shell of a costume, and short little arms, into a living, vehemently mobile being, and at the same time to give it a precise, typical and unmistakeable character.

Only the upper part of the body is visible, as with a person seen at a window. Often such a puppet also has a single leg or pair of legs which are swung high-spiritedly over the front of the stage and dangle indolently when the figure, facing the public, sits down on the playboard. The operator works the puppet directly with his hand, which he inserts from below the figure, so that his forefinger moves the head and his thumb and middle finger (or, even better, little finger) the two arms.

Thanks to the almost complete identification of hand and puppet, a most impressive and, in the truest sense of the word, gripping effect is achieved.

Participation by the spectators, who are encouraged to interject comments to which the puppeteer instantly reacts, makes possible a contact with the public, which no other form of puppetry can attain. The special popularity achieved by hand puppets in street and fairground shows is due to their primitive directness, which appeals above all to children and simple natures, and to their uncomplicated equipment, permitting this type of puppet to make shift with the most improvised of pitches.

The hand puppets' spectacular chief character is the cunning Kasperl, to be found all over Europe in many national or regional variations, such as Pulcinella, Polichinelle and Guignol, Punch or Petrushka. This irrepressible descendant of Hanswurst invariably behaves as a pugnacious and frequently unscrupulous clown, at the same time embodying, as a kind of catalyst of public opinion, the principle of what is just and right, which is always in danger. With the freedom allowed to a jester and by means of improvised social-critical tirades, he imperturbably interprets what everyone is thinking but never dares to say out loud.

Kasperl's natural counterparts in the puppet theatre are the Devil, Death, the Witch, the Robbers and the Policeman. The Policeman, the symbol of authority, oppression and imprisonment, was possibly the greatest object of fear for travelling people, among whom the puppeteers were once numbered.

The earliest information about hand puppetry in Europe stems from the Middle Ages. A picture by Jehan de Grise in a manuscript (probably Flemish of 1338 to 1344 and now in the Oxford Bodleian Library) of the *Roman du bon roi Alexandre* suggests that it already had more fastidious devotees.

The simple and popular appeal of hand puppetry has not prevented the modern artistic puppet theatre from making use of this vital and lively medium, which allows the puppeteer to exploit every incident and inspiration of the moment. In the process, the traditional and established characters have been superseded by others, more refined and psychologically more complex.

16 GIRL OF THE BIEDERMEIER PERIOD

Munich, c. 1860.

A hand puppet, formerly belonging to Josef Leonhard Schmid, known as "Papa Schmid" (born 1822 at Amberg; died 1912 in Munich). Used for occasional private performances.

Materials: wood and textile; intact in original condition.

Height: 54 cm.

The figure has a rosy, doll-like face framed in black hair, and a conical bonnet. The dress is light, with a Turkish pattern trimmed with lace. Red and light blue stockings. Black leather shoes.

17 DAME A LA MODE

Munich. The head is about 1860. The clothing is probably of a later date.

A hand puppet, formerly belonging to "Papa Schmid".

Wood and textile. Intact in original condition.

Height: 50 cm.

A ladylike blonde, from a parody on portrait-painting, in the style of a man-

nequin doll of the 1860s. She wears a huge red hat, with a conspicuous display of flowers, ostrich feathers and silk ribbons, and a spring-green costume with black lace. Her legs are covered with many-coloured stockings and brown shoes.

18 KASPERL

Munich. About 1925.

From the Kasperl theatre of Toni Schmid (1882–1949).

Wood and textile. Roughly and clumsily executed.

Height: 65 cm.

A peasant, artful and sly, with a long nose in the manner of a "Dumme August" (clown). He wears a blue linen jacket, a white shirt, black green-striped trousers, red children's shoes and a green "Geissbuben" (goatsherd's) hat. The figure has one leg.

The showman, Toni Schmid, was born at Straubing and served an apprenticeship as a locksmith and mechanic; he later settled in Munich. He also worked marionettes. Other popular hand-puppet theatres in Munich have included those of:

Johann Eisen (1877–1955), Karl Birkenmeier (1883–1957), Hans Schmid senr (1884, still performing), Karl Dehner (1898–1968) and Josef Kiebl (1901–1970). Kasperl is the successor of the Hanswurst of the farces of the Baroque age. He was banished from the theatre at Leipzig by "Die Neuberin" (Frederika Carolina Neuber, an actress-manageress of the first half of the eighteenth century) at the instigation of the literary critic, Johann Christoph Gottsched, who sought to reform the German stage. The jester-buffoon survived in the Austrian theatre, thanks to the players Stranitzky and Prehauser, and towards the end of the eighteenth century the Viennese popular comedian, Laroche, achieved new fame for him. In Salzburg peasant dress and later mostly in regional costume, Kasperl conquered the German theatre. There he became a central figure, naïve yet brave, embodying all human weaknesses and enjoying the unreserved affection and love of the public.

19 KASPER
Hohnstein (Saxony). About 1930.
From the artistic hand-puppet theatre founded by Max Jacob (1888–1967) at Hartenstein, subsequently based at Hohnstein.
Carved by Theo Eggink.
Height: 68 cm.
A beaming, laughing face, with a big hook nose, protruding chin and blue eyes. The jacket is brown, patterned, edged with braid and worn over a light shirt with a lace collar. The figure has legs.
This puppet won Max Jacob a Gold Medal in 1937 at the Paris World Exhibition. Hand puppetry received new and

continuing impetus from Jacob as a result of the Hohnstein style which he developed. From 1957 till his death he was President of UNIMA (Union Internationale de la Marionnette).

20 GUIGNOL
Lyons. About the start of this century.
Wood and textile. Renovated.
Height: 53 cm.
A boyish, saucy face, with light-pink colouring and large dark eyes. He wears the dress of a Lyons silk weaver—a brown jacket and waistcoat with a black coat, and a kind of cap on his head with the suggestion of a pigtail.
Guignol, who speaks in street jargon created by Laurent Mourguet (1745 to 1844), became so popular in France that other puppet theatres adopted him as their chief character, rather than the traditional Polichinelle.

21 PUNCH
England. End of the nineteenth century.
From William Davis's Punch and Judy theatre (London).
Wood and textile. Original condition.
Height: 65 cm.
A rowdy brute, ferociously jovial, with a piercing gaze, bared teeth and a nose with a fiery red tip which sticks out. He wears a red dress with a bright ruffle and a horn-shaped red cap.
William Davis appeared on the London streets for over forty years with this Punch, his dog playing Toby.
The name Punch is an anglicization of Pulcinella or Punchinello. His 300th birthday was celebrated in the Covent Garden district of London on 26 May 1962, where, according to an entry in Samuel Pepys' *Diary*, he made his debut in 1662. Initially he was something of a loud-mouthed woman-chaser and Jonathan Swift attributed the popularity of Punch, who delivers as many blows as he receives, to his impudence and shamelessness.

22 LASLO VITEZ
Hungary. End of the nineteenth century.
From Hendrik Kemény's hand-puppet theatre, Budapest.

From "Kasperl in Turkey", one of the Kasperl Comedies of Count Franz Pocci

Wood and textile. Original condition.
Height: 56 cm.

A bull-like very brown face, with round red cheeks, a snub nose, black hair, a pointed cap and dark red clothes. The coat has braiding sewn on it, and the figure has legs.

Lásló Vitéz, Kasperl's cousin and, in the most literal sense, a quick-witted daredevil, is the traditional hero of Hungarian popular puppetry. In order to rid himself of his opponents he resorts, not to cudgels or blows, but to one of his many frying pans.

23 VASILACHE (Little Basilius)
Rumania. Nineteenth century.
Wood and textile.
Height: 60 cm.

A primitively-carved and painted face, with the cheeks and nose emphasized. The moustache has been glued on. The green jelly-bag head covering, worn to one side, has red buttons. The sack-like dress is red. This is a rare figure since many such puppets were confiscated and burnt as symbols of rebellion, because of Vasilache's criticism of political and social conditions.

The Fair at Cannstadt, by Johann M. Voltz, 1835

24 JAN KLAASSEN
(Jan Claez, Jan Claeszen, Jan Klaaszoon)
Holland. Start of the present century.
From an unknown Dutch popular hand-puppet theatre.
Wood and textile.
Height: 65 cm.
Strongly stylized, with a rigid, rose-coloured face and a peaked hat bent forward, in a sack-like, sand-coloured velvet costume.
Jan Klaassen is said to have been a trumpeter in the service of the Stadholder Prince Willem II in about the year 1650 and, after the latter's death, to have become a puppeteer in Amsterdam, his native city. According to tradition he portrayed himself in this figure.
See: *Doopceel van Jan Claeszen* by Wim Meilink, Amsterdam 1969.

25 GRETL
Munich. About 1925.
From the Kasperl theatre of Toni Schmid (1882–1949).
Wood and textile. Original state.
Height: 49 cm.
A naïve face, with staring eyes ringed by eyelashes. The cheeks and chin are red-tinted. The black hair has been painted on. The bonnet is dark and speckled and the dress and apron are sprigged.
Gretl is Kasperl's wife and companion. In the hand-puppet show she figures more in Kasperl's words than she actually participates in the proceedings.

26 JUDY
England. End of the nineteenth century.
From an unknown London Punch and Judy show.
Wood and textile. Original state.
Height: 43 cm.
A silly, quarrelsome female. She has a large nose, a broad arched chin and a scolding open mouth. The dress and cap are yellow, ornamented with lilac lace.
Judy is Punch's wife. Previously known as Joan, the change in the name came with the introduction of the "swazzle" (small metal plates bound together), "Judy" being easier to say. Whereas the performer gives Punch's voice a nasal intonation with the aid of the swazzle, he speaks the role of Judy normally. A Punch and Judy booth is also referred to as a "swazzle box".

27 KATRINTJE
Holland. Start of the present century.
From an unknown popular Jan Klaassen theatre.
Wood and textile. Coarsely executed.
Height: 42 cm.
An artless, surly person, with a pink painted face and red cheeks. The white bonnet covers her ears. Trimmed with lace, her light blue dress has a motif of white flowers.
She partners Jan Klaassen. She may represent Katrintje Pieters, real wife of the trumpeter, Jan Klaassen.
See: *Doopceel van Jan Claeszen* by Wim Meilink, Amsterdam 1969.

28 DEVIL
France. End of the nineteenth century.
From an unknown popular hand-puppet theatre in Lyons.
Wood and textile. Fine original state in red.
Height: 55 cm.
A fire-red head with protruding ears and a tongue which sticks out. The eyes are button-shaped and glisten. The closely-fitting headgear has built-in horns. The clothing is also red.

29 PRINCE (also shown on cover)
Munich. Start of the present century.
From Toni Schmid's Kasperl theatre.
Wood and textile. Original state.
Height: 55 cm.
In the style of an archaic ruler, with a direct, stern gaze. The face is brownish with a heavy, reddish beard and a patterned cap turned down at one side. The costume is of olive-green velvet.

30 A SMITH
Munich. Start of the present century.
From Toni Schmid's Kasperl theatre.
Wood, textile and leather. Original condition.
Height: 49 cm.
A choleric character. The eyes are wide open; below the moustache the protruding teeth fully exposed. He has an upturned peak to his cap and a black coat with white pinstripes. The leather apron is brittle.

31 CIVILIAN AND SOLDIER

Munich. Nineteenth century.

From the Kasperl theatre of Johann Eisen (1877–1955).

Wood and textile. In their original state, but badly damaged through use.

Height: 56 cm.

Roughly made figures. The one on the left is a good-for-nothing, with crafty eyes, a pointed beard, a green hunter's coat with many buttons and a brown tasselled cap. The other is a private soldier, used to being ordered about, in a cap without a peak but with cockades. The green uniform has red piping. The figure is one-legged.

Johann Eisen belonged to a family of South German puppeteers which can be traced back to about 1810.

32 EXTENDABLE MAN

Munich. About 1870.

From the family theatre of Lothar Meggendorfer (1847–1925).

Wood and textile. In excellent original state.

Height: 49 cm.

A moustached Pandour (Austrian soldier) with a hooked nose. The fur cap forms part of the head. The costume including the jacket is dark red with brown stripes, together with colourful accessories and a white ruffle. By means of a stick the concertina-like neck can be extended and the figure greatly enlarged. It has feet.

Lothar Meggendorfer was a contributor to the Munich comic illustrated broadsides, the *Münchner Bilderbogen*, published by the firm of Braun und Schneider. He also founded the humorous weekly journal, the *Meggendorfer Blätter*, which was amalgamated with the *Fliegende Blätter* (another humorous paper) in 1928.

33 A NOBLEMAN

Italian, from Cremona. 1864.

From the Burattini theatre of Ernesto Tortiroli.

Wood and textile. Original state, but damaged.

Height: 45 cm.

A classically shaped male head with moustache and side whiskers. The hair is of black material, and the costume is yellow.

The Italian term Burattini, applicable to this figure, refers exclusively to hand puppets. Already in use before the Commedia dell'Arte called one of its characters Burattino, it has changed its meaning in the course of time.

34 VAMP

Zurich. 1947.

From the artistic hand-puppet theatre of Fred Schneckenburger (1901–66).

Wood, textile and other materials.

Height: 53 cm.

A blonde, with a lilac-tinted face and yellowish and brown feathers on her head. The costume is violet with multi-coloured ruches and lace insertions.

The figure is magically transformed from a crocodile into a vamp. The Swiss puppet-maker and puppeteer, Fred Schneckenburger, through his surrealist creations became one of the boldest pioneers of the modern puppet theatre.

35 MINISTER AND GOSSIP ("Chatty Kathy")

Munich. 1925.

From Tilly Gaissmaier and Max Pokorny's artistic hand-puppet theatre.

Wood and textile.

Height: 58 and 50 cm.

Left: A jovial senior official in a dark red uniform with a high collar and a black coat and hat. The figure has one leg.

Right: A talkative old lady in a rose-coloured dress with a black straw bonnet and a working mouth.

Tilly Gaissmaier made her debut in 1926, with figures carved by Max Pokorny, at the Steinicke-Saal in Munich. Both were representative of the artistic flair for puppetry in the 1920s.

36 MAID SERVANT (from *Don Perlimplin* by F. Garcia Lorca)

Rome. About 1952.

From Maria Signorelli's *Opera dei Burattini*.

Textile and papier mâché.

Height: 80 cm.

A ghostly apparition, with a distorted terrified face. The hands are stretched out like claws. The loosely-hanging costume is composed of violet, green, rose-

From "Punch and Judy", by George Cruikshank, 1828

coloured and black silk rags. There is also a net-like dark lilac cloak. The green taffeta hat is crumpled.

Maria Signorelli, Roman puppeteer and theatre historian, aims at a "fantastic resuscitation of something imperishable, and human — that is tradition, as represented by the puppet theatre."

Marionettes

Marionettes, though related to hand puppets, are delicate, poetic and artificial in comparison with the rough vitality of hand puppets. Even the Sicilian knight marionettes, which after bloody skirmishes end up as piles of corpses littering the stage, possess an air of chivalrous distinction.

The word 'marionette' denotes in French, from which it is derived, every form of theatrical puppet. In France it is spelt 'marionnette' (that is, with two 'ns', unlike the practice in other countries). International puppet terminology, however, reserves the appellation exclusively for puppets suspended on iron rods or strings.

The operator works his marionette from above by means of a crosspiece (often called a 'crutch' or 'perch') to which all the strings are attached. This he lifts, lowers, tilts and turns, with the addition of a system of supplementary aids varying in complexity. Thus equipped, a skilled puppeteer can achieve wonders in simulating life.

A puppet, whether made of wood, textiles, wires and papier-mâché or, as nowadays, of synthetic materials, can carry out a variety of inter-related movements, which suggest a real or imaginary being so convincingly that, if dexterously manipulated, it will stand comparison in every way with a flesh-and-blood actor, sometimes even surpassing the latter's attainments in the field of illusion. The traditional travelling marionette theatres right up to the present century had, in fact, no other ambition than to imitate the 'live' theatre.

After the banishment of Hanswurst from the German stage of the Gottsched era, the travelling theatres continued the tradition of the Baroque popular theatre, with its repertoire of plays about knightly gallantry, melodramas and ghost stories, its broad sentimental style, and its seemingly magical transformation scenes and effects.

The indecent jokes of the funny characters and the low standards of morality and culture compelled censors to prohibit scenes and even to prosecute individual puppeteers. But the mannered and theatrical form of delivery and style of performance remained unchanged for generations in many showmen's families.

In a few fortunate cases the entire inventory has survived, right up to our own times. This consists of the complete stage equipment, weighing many hundred-weights, made up of scenery and backcloths, which roll up and down, and side wings, together with a collection of comparatively few unclothed figures which, dressed and undressed and with exchangeable heads, may be converted into whatever role is required.

56 A Turk
19th century trick figure
From Adolf Winter's marionette theatre
of Kevelaer
(colour plate III)

59   Harlequin
Munich, 1866
From Schmid's marionette theatre
(colour plate IV)

62 The Marquis Castipiani among
the Girls
Baden-Baden, 1920
From Ivo Puhonny's marionette theatre
(colour plate V)

82   Magic lantern
19th century
(colour plate VI)

The history of the marionette can be traced beyond that of the hand puppet, back to the fifth century B. C. and its Greek terracotta figures with jointed limbs, though these might, of course, have been children's playthings.

Our knowledge of the early days of the marionette is based solely on incidental references in Greek literature, which certainly confirm the existence of puppeteers, and indeed of marionette performers, if the word *neurospast* may be translated as 'string-puller'. But they give no explanation as to the manner and character of puppetry in the ancient world.

The name marionette, already in use by the seventeenth century, in the sense of *marionnette à fils* (a puppet controlled from above, a string puppet), is believed to have come from a French thirteenth-century pastorale, the *Jeu de Robin et Marion*, in which 'Marionnette' occurs as a pet name.

The term also appears to be closely associated with the movable figures of the Virgin Mary of mediaeval Christmas cribs. This theory tends to be confirmed by the existence at one time in Paris of the street, the 'rue des marionnettes', where objects of piety were sold (including 'marioles', 'little Maries' or figurines of the Virgin Mary).

In Germany it is only in the sixteenth century that information about puppeteers begins to accumulate in any quantity, thanks to the city council records. These reveal their names (as, for example, that of Hainrichen von Burgunde who was refused permission on 14 June 1510 to perform his *Tockelspiel* of the Passion of Our Lord). It is also possible to reconstruct from them many of the itineraries of the showmen.

Marionettes found their way as a kind of cultivated pastime in the eighteenth century into the palaces of Venetian patricians and into the courts of Europe. The puppet theatre at Prince Esterhazy's castle at Eisenstadt in the Austrian Burgenland province, for which Haydn, who was the Prince's musical director, wrote several operas, was held in such high esteem that the Empress herself, Maria Theresa, asked for it to appear at her Palace of Schönbrunn.

Goethe's *Faust* takes as its source the old puppet play of that name known to have been first produced in 1588 at Tübingen, and the nature of the marionette theatre appealed to the Romantics, who enthusiastically amassed all the orally transmitted treasures of popular literature they could.

It was the Bavarian count, Franz Pocci, who established marionettes firmly in the world of entertainment. In 1858 the Count enabled Josef Leonhard Schmid, later known as 'Papa Schmid', then working in a clerical capacity in Munich, to establish a permanent marionette theatre, for which he wrote, in romantic and ironic spirit, nearly fifty puppet comedies. With their enchanting mixture of fairy tale and satire they remain to this day part of the classical repertoire of the puppet theatre. This happy co-operation between the art-loving Count and Papa Schmid was an exemplary prelude to the subsequent collaboration, realized as essential, between puppeteers and good writers. Similarly it led to the artistic reassessment of the puppets themselves, on whose production important sculptors and artists were from that point to be employed.

37   A POSTER (detail)

Sicily. End of the nineteenth century.
From Francesco Sclafani's Marionette Theatre at Palermo.
Distemper, on canvas.
Size: 192 by 138 cm. (complete).
Three of eight scenes on a poster painted in the manner of German "Moritaten-bilder". The subjects represented are the oath-taking ceremony of Ginamo and Beatrice and the deaths of Ruggiero Milone and Almonte.

38   STAGE CURTAIN

Sicily. End of the nineteenth century.
From Francesco Sclafani's Marionette Theatre at Palermo.
Distemper, on canvas.
Size: 175 by 235 cm.
A dramatic depiction of the uprising of the people of Palermo against the officials of Charles I of Anjou on Easter Monday 1282. The massacre achieved tragic fame, becoming known as the Sicilian Vespers.

39   A DEVIL

Sicily. Nineteenth century.
From an unknown *Opera dei Pupi* (probably of Taormina).
Wood, fur and canvas.
Height: 90 cm.
A massive head, with a voluminous nose and an open mouth like that of an animal, with the tongue hanging out. The upper part of the body is exposed, with a sheepskin loincloth. The colours are rose and red. As with all Sicilian marionettes, the figure is suspended from an iron rod, fixed vertically to the head.

40   GIANTS

Sicily. Nineteenth century.
From Francesco Sclafani's Marionette Theatre, at Palermo.
Wood and textile.
Height: 90 to 95 cm.
Barone, Ternau and Rominante, so-called giants. Moustached warriors, with turban-like head coverings and wide breeches of an oriental style. They have swords but no armour.

41   THE BATTLE OF RONCEVALLES (detail)

A reconstruction of a scene from the *Opera dei Pupi*.
Sicily. Nineteenth century.
From theatres at Catania and Acireale.
The curtains and scenery: canvas and painted wood; the marionettes: wood, velvet, silk, linen, feathers, braiding and edgings, also metal.
Height of the figures: 135 to 140 cm.
The figures have magnificent costumes and artistically embossed armour. They represent Paladins and Saracens, characters in the *Song of Roland* which tells of the heroic deeds of the knights of Christendom when, as the rearguard of Charlemagne, they were betrayed and ambushed by the Saracens in the Valley of Roncevalles in the year 778.
The puppets weigh over half a hundredweight and are operated by iron rods. The stage is frequently completely covered with corpses in chaotic heaps. The characters are taken from the world of the legends of the Crusades described in Ariosto's *Orlando Furioso* and Torquato Tasso's *Gerusalemme Liberata*.
According to a romantic story, this type of marionette was brought from Naples (where there were already references to them in 1646) to Sicily in the nineteenth century in the wake of the *Risorgimento* by the actor Giovanni Grassi who successfully escaped, after a series of adventures, from Bourbon police.
The Sicilian marionette theatre has achieved fresh fame as a tourist attraction. Its main centres are at Palermo and Acireale and in Catania.

42   THE BATTLE OF RONCEVALLES

A complete picture of the reconstructed scene.

43   POPULAR TYPES

Liége (Belgium). Nineteenth century.
From a Tchantchès theatre.
Wood and textiles. Original state.
Height: 75 cm.
Grotesque people with distorted anatomical features, such as an elongated head or an excessively protruding nose.

Playbill-programme for J. Schmid's Marionetten-theater at Munich. Sunday 23 September 1883. (Double bill, consisting of "Hansel and Gretel" or "The Man-Eater" and "The Water and Fire Test" or "Kasperl as Wonder Doctor")

J. Schmid's Marionetten-Theater
im Klenzegarten,
Klenzestraße Nro. 36, nächst dem Theater am Gärtnerplatz.
Sonntag, den 23. September 1883.

Hansel und Grethel
oder
Der Menschenfresser.

Dramatisches Märchen in 2 Aufzügen von Franz Pocci.

Personen:

Peter, ein armer Holzhauer.
Marianne, dessen Weib.
Hansel, ihre Kinder.
Grethel,
Professor Doktor Fleischmann, Naturforscher und Menschen-
fresser.
Katharine, dessen Haushälterin.
Casperl Larisari, wandernder Schneidergeselle.
Schnauzbart, Gerichtsdiener.
Die Nacht.
Der Mond.

Hierauf:

Die Wasser- und Feuer-Probe
oder
Casperl als Wunderdoktor.

Zauberdrama in 3 Aufzügen mit Gesang von Dr. K . . .

Personen:

Al Gorab, ein Magier.	Rathsdiener.
Mystifar, ein Zauberer, anfänglich in Gestalt eines Pfaues.	Ein Gendarme.
Lucrezia, dessen Tochter.	Ragozzi, ein indianischer Priester.
Casperl.	Guli, dessen Tochter.
Bürgermeister.	Indianer.

Preise der Plätze:

Reservirter Platz 60 Pfennige, zweiter Platz 40 Pfennige, dritter Platz 20 Pfennige.

Billets sind an der Theaterkasse im Laufe des Vormittags zu haben und sind dieselben nur für den Tag, an welchem
sie gelöst wurden, giltig.

Anfang Nachmittags halb 4 Uhr. Ende 3/4 6 Uhr.

Das Theater wird um 3 Uhr geöffnet.

The Tchantchès figures represent the popular Walloon theatre in Belgium. The most important collection of the kind, at the Musée de la Vie Wallonne at Liége, belongs to the Théâtre Pinet. In addition to the religious crib-theatre figures and the romantic heroes of the Roland saga and other classic poems, there are invariably heavily-caricatured characters of everyday life. The public takes joy in recognizing itself in these.

44 A BURGHER
Brussels. Mid-nineteenth century.
From a Toone theatre.
Wood and fabric. Original state.
Height: 100 cm.
A comfortably-off gentleman, whose clothes are very stylish but also very much the worse for wear.
The traditional and purely Flemish Toone theatre goes back to 1812 and is concentrated mainly on Brussels, as well as Antwerp and Lille.

45 PALADINS AND SARACEN
Liége. Nineteenth century.
From a Tchantchès theatre.
Wood and fabric.
Height: 75 to 80 cm.
These are warriors from the cast of the Roland saga, resembling in looks and performance the larger Sicilian iron-rod marionettes. Their armour and helmets are not of metal but of carved wood, often richly ornamented.

46 A NOBLEMAN
Czechoslovakia. Second half of the nineteenth century.
From an unknown travelling marionette theatre.
Wood and fabric. In excellent, original condition.
Height: 75 cm.
A good-natured, distinguished and paternal aristocrat. His coat and trousers are of violet silk with lace, and he wears a biretta-like cap. At the top end of the controlling iron rod is a bound handle, typical of old Czech marionettes.
Czechoslovakia has a distinctive puppetry tradition. Developed in times of cultural repression, it formed the basis for the present pre-eminent position occupied by the nation's puppet theatres.

47 KASPERL AND TWO FRIENDS
Austria. Second half of the nineteenth century.
The figures on the left and right are from the Staud travelling marionette theatre of Krems. The origin of the Kasperl figure (the one in the middle) is not known.
Wood and textile.
Height: 61 to 71 cm.
An artisan, Kasperl and a disabled trader. They are typical popular characters, executed in an extremely realistic manner. Kasperl has a red carnival costume and several gaps in his teeth. His right-hand neighbour has only one arm. Warts, wrinkles and other blemishes have been carefully noted.

48 INHABITANTS OF HADES
Colour plate I
Austria. Nineteenth century.
From an East Bohemian travelling marionette theatre.
Wood and textile.
Height: 40 to 71 cm.
Four different Devils and Death.
These fearsome symbols of the torments of Hell and eternal damnation are important metaphysical characters of the popular theatre whose roots, which have an element of nightmare about them, reach back to the thinking of the Middle Ages.
The devils and the backcloth are probably part of an old version of *Doctor Faustus*.

49 SOME OF THE BEST PEOPLE
England. End of the eighteenth century.
From an unknown marionette theatre.
Wood and textile, with real hair. Original state.
Height: 50 to 63 cm
These are string puppets, fashionably and extravagantly costumed in the style of the "live" theatre, as courtiers and members of the aristocracy. The face of the kneeling nobleman looks almost Shakespearean. The girl's clothes and stance are doll-like. The figures might well have been used for a number of roles.

50 CLOWN
Colour plate II
England. Early nineteenth century.
From an unknown marionette theatre.
Wood and textile. Original state.
Height: 62 cm.
The make-up and costume (with lilac-coloured, bespangled ornamentation on a white background, and red stockings) in all probability derive from Joseph Grimaldi, the great Regency clown and pantomimist. The puppet's right hand is closed and hollowed out (for holding objects). The thumb of the left hand is movable.

51 DEVIL
South Germany. Nineteenth century.
From Johann Jungkunz's travelling marionette theatre.
Wood and textile. In original state.
Height: 90 cm.
A grinning black devil with diminutive ears and horns. The skirt and neck-frill are red, with red rosettes on the body. From an old *Faust* play.
Johann Jungkunz, born between 1860 and 1880, as a child accompanied his father who was a horse-dealer and Kasperl performer. At the age of seventeen he went as a groom to the well-known puppeteer, Ernst Lehner, often called "der alte Eisen" ("Old Iron"). He soon became the latter's assistant and learned his trade. Jungkunz mainly toured Lower Bavaria.

52 BEARDED NOBLEMAN
South Germany. Nineteenth century.
From Johann Jungkunz's travelling marionette theatre.
Wood and textile. Original state.
Height: 92 cm.
A strongly stylized, expressive head, with a frightening look and protruding glass eyes.

53 A JOLLY GIRL
Central Germany. Start of the present century.
From the Strohbusch travelling marionette theatre of Halle.
Wood and textile.
Height: 70 cm.
An innocent, sentimental blonde. A contracted face, with a low brow and a large nose. Truly naïve.

54 A LITTLE DEVIL
South Germany. Nineteenth century.
From Johann Jungkunz's travelling marionette theatre.
Wood and fur. Evidence of age and use.
Height: 80 cm.
A bizarre figure, with fiendish eyes, goat horns and serrated teeth, a black head and a body of shabby fur.

55 "DER GLOCKENGUSS ZU BRESLAU"
(The Bell-Cast at Breslau)
North Germany. Nineteenth century.
From Adolf Winter's marionette theatre, Kevelaer.
Wood and textile.
Height (of the figures): 93 cm.
An original scene from this ambulant theatre which, preserved complete with all its equipment, has been set up at the Munich Puppet Theatre Collection. Part of the proscenium of the Jungkunz Theatre has been used.
These are romantically-costumed and stiffly ethereal characters, in highly theatrical poses. Kneeling in the centre, in a green velvet and silk costume, is Anna, daughter of the bell-founder, with (left) the gentle Senator, Werhardt. On the right in a plain smock, the picture of remorse and magnanimity, is Konstantin Helm, the bell-founder.
Adolf Winter (1886–1967) was born at Hohenauen in Westhavelland, and died at Eppenhain in the Rhineland. He was the son of Karl Winter, who travelled in Schleswig-Holstein with a Mechanisches Kunstfigurentheater. The Winter family are believed to have been puppeteers from the sixteenth century.

56 A TURK (trick figure)
Colour plate III
North Germany. Nineteenth century.
From Adolf Winter's marionette theatre of Kevelaer.
Wood and textile.
Height: 58 cm.
The figure is first seen as a Turk, magnificently attired in red and black, with a turban on his head.

A string is pulled and the turban immediately opens revealing, as it falls down over the Turk's face, the head of a woman who, in the same instant, holds four children by the hand.

Metamorphoses (as these trick figures were called — and the Turk is a typical example) were a constant source of amazement to the public. They served to fill in the intervals between scene changes and often showmen concluded their programmes by exhibiting them.

57 A KNIGHT AND HIS LADY

Berchtesgaden (Bavaria). End of the nineteenth century.
From the Gailler-Walch marionette theatre.
Wood, textile and metal. Original state.
Height: 98 cm.
Fairy-tale characters of mannered and romantic nobility. One is a lord with a regal bearing, a grand plume and a well-groomed Henry IV beard. He has a black velvet, silver-braided cloak over his silver-lamé armour. The other is a great lady, tall and imposing, in a rose silk dress, trimmed with lace and braid. These figures, of great quality, were probably carved at Oberammergau.

Gabriel Gailler (died 1917 — his origin is not known) was at various times an ambulance man, a hawker, a guitar player, a ventriloquist and the owner of a marionette theatre, which he sold in 1906 for 800 marks to his partner, Ludwig Walch (1881–1911). On the death of Walch, who had also been a scene painter, a musician and a Bavarian folk dancer (a Schuhplattler), his widow and later his son, Ludwig Walch junr., continued with the theatre, touring the Berchtesgaden area and the Salzkammergut (Austria) until 1936. Ludwig Walch junr. was also known as a crib-figure carver.

58 BIOS AND TWO GENIUSES

Munich. 1869.
From Schmid's marionette theatre.
(Papa Schmid, 1822–1912).
Wax, wood and textile.
Height: 30 cm.
The figures are for a magic play, *Das Glück ist blind oder Kasperl im Schuld-turm* (Fortune is Blind or Kasperl in the Debtor's Prison) by Franz Pocci, with music by Hans Hager, first performed on 7 March 1869.

Bios, the spirit of life, has a garland of flowers and a tulle costume. The two geniuses have wax heads, like those for crib figures, and the sort of wings with which the ballerina, Maria Taglioni, was to become world famous as La Sylphide. Josef Leonhard Schmid, known as "Papa Schmid," a bookbinder by trade, was subsequently employed with the Unterstützungsverein für das Amts- und Kanzleipersonal (Officials and Clerks Benevolent Association). With the help of Count Franz Pocci, a brilliant all-round amateur, he started Munich's first permanent marionette theatre with which the epoch of artistic puppetry began. In 1911 Papa Schmid handed the theatre over to his daughter, Babette Klinger. On her death Karl Winkler carried it on up to 1934.

(See the Catalogue of the Papa Schmid Exhibition of the Puppentheatersammlung der Stadt München, 1967).

59 HARLEQUIN

Colour plate IV
Munich, 1866.
From Schmid's marionette theatre.
Wood and textile.
Height: 30 cm.
Harlequin, with traces of the Commedia dell'Arte, from *Der Fasching in München im Jahre 1563 oder die Entstehung des Schäfflertanzes* (Carnival in Munich in 1563 or The Origin of the Cooper's Dance), a carnival farce by Cesar Max Heigel.

60 GOETHE EXAMINED

Munich. About 1925.
From Paul Brann's Marionettentheater Münchner Künstler (Munich Artists' Marionette Theatre).
Wood and textile.
Height: 63 to 75 cm.
Olaf Gulbransson made these figures for Alfred Polgar's and Egon Friedell's satirical sketch, *Goethe im Examen*, which brought the German professor-type down from the lofty position generally assigned to him. Such caricatured dramatists as Ibsen and Gerhard Hauptmann, no longer contemporaries, were similarly treated.

Protesting spectators. About 1800, anonymous

Between 1906 and 1934, the year he emigrated to Britain, the actor and author, Paul Brann, showed the way modern puppetry should develop. He gave concrete form to the plan for an artistic marionette theatre, in which there was close co-operation between a group of well-known poets and theatre people, painters, sculptors and musicians.

61 HARLEQUIN AND COLUMBINE
Munich. 1925.
By Max Pokorny.
Wood and textile.
Height: 50 to 52 cm.
Solo marionettes as a pair of dancers, in the manner of the later phase of "Jugendstil" (art nouveau).
In the 1920s the puppet-maker, Max Pokorny, working with Tilly Gaissmaier who designed the costumes, gained a reputation which spread far beyond Munich.

62 THE MARQUIS CASTIPIANI AMONG THE GIRLS
Colour plate V
Baden-Baden. 1920.
From Ivo Puhonny's Baden-Badener Künstler-Marionetten-Theater (Baden-Baden Artistic Marionette Theatre).
Wood and textile.
Height: 51 to 58 cm.

A degenerate marquis with a group of girls dancing the Charleston, from a production of Wedekind's play *Tod und Teufel* (Death and the Devil) which was banned after its first performance. In 1911 Ivo Puhonny (1876–1940), a well-known commercial artist and a man of the world with artistic leanings, who was greatly influenced by a tour of Asia, established a marionette theatre in the Palais Hamilton. He toured Europe and many other parts of the world with an elaborate literary programme.

33

63 SIGNALS IN SHADOW
Paris. 1955–9.
By Harry Kramer (born 1925 at
Lingen/Ems).
Metal and plastic substance.
Height: 52 cm.
Harry Kramer's wheeled figure is a cross
between a machine and a pre-historic island idol. His mechanical theatre shows
the marionette strangely alienated from
its traditional form, tending to develop
plasticity but with its movements as precisely controlled as before.
Trained as an actor, dancer and choreo-
grapher, Harry Kramer lives in Paris and
is a sculptor and film-maker.

64 THE RASCAL GIRON AND
A SOLDIER
Stockholm. 1964.
From Michael Meschke's Marionetteatern.
Plywood.
Height: 88 and 104 cm.
Flat figures, designed by Franciska The-
merson of London for a production of
Alfred Jarry's *Ubu Roi*. This production
– in purely graphic, two-dimensional and
black-and-white terms, with a homo-
genous ensemble of masked actors and
mechanical figures – was Michael Meschke's break-through, a development important not only in the puppet theatre.
Meschke cites as a source of inspiration
for both performance and direction Harry
Kramer's mechanical theatre, which is
based on "simple principles of movement
[as in] Jumping Jacks, the pendulum and
the technique of primitive toys".

65 FLORINDE, THE LADY
WITHOUT AN ABDOMEN
Brunswick. 1961.
From Harro Siegel's marionette theatre.
Various substances and textile.
Height: 80 cm.
A lady in a low-cut dress, whose bosom
rests on an occasional table. In the
Museum of Curiosities of Wilhelm von
Scholz's "Doppelkopf" (The Double
Head).
Harro M. Siegel, born 1900, is a creator
of puppets, in whom formal artistic in-

vention and epigrammatic pictorial hu-
mour are combined with a refined sense
of the constructive and the mechanical.
He has also rendered immense service as
a teacher at the Brunswick Werkschule
(Technical College) and as the organiser
of the city's International Puppet Festi-
vals.

66 BEFORE MIDNIGHT
Berlin. 1966.
From the Hochschule für bildende Kün-
ste, Klasse "Spiel und Bühne", of Professor Herta Schönewolf (Petra Mimkes).
(The "Play and Stage" Class of Professor
Herta Schönewolf [Petra Mimkes] at the
West Berlin College of Art and Design).
Metal.
Height: 61 to 70 cm.
These marionettes show humans as though
in an X-ray picture, in the metaphorical
style of Arcimboldo. The skeletons, and
particularly the one with the mechanism
of a clock for a face, resemble figures in
a dance of death.
These scrap-metal combinations, made
from junk and cynically estranged from
their original purpose, could well sym-
bolize all that is fleeting and transient in
human life.

67 MISS HACKIT
Munich. 1936.
From Hilmar Binter's marionette theatre.
Wood and textile.
Height: 64 cm.
This figure of Miss Hackit, lean, with
buck teeth and a pointed nose, was iron-
ically created by the sculptor Walter
Oberholzer. It was made specially for
Forster-Burggraf's play about Daniel De-
foe, *Robinson soll nicht sterben* (Robinson Shall not Die).
Oberholzer, a Swiss resident in Munich
from 1915, assisted by his wife Lise who
made the costumes, designed and produced about 600 figures for the Binter theatre
between 1924 and 1950. His work, which
is always unmistakable, portrays everyday types with a wit reminiscent of
Daumier.

83   Magic lantern
19th century
(colour plate VII)

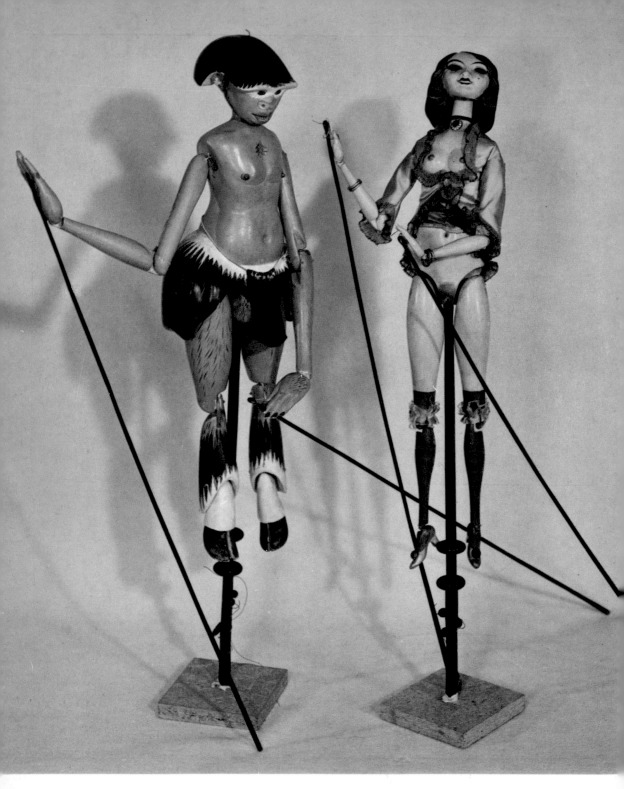

71   Faun and nymph
Rod puppets, 1914
By Richard Teschner, Vienna
(colour plate VIII)

Rod Puppets

By virtue of its qualities and what it achieves, the rod puppet occupies a place between the hand puppet and the marionette. While it has much of the directness and vitality of the one, it has also the complicated charm and subtle individuality of the other.

As with the hand puppet the rod puppet is worked from below, both hands of the operator being involved. One holds up the figure on its pole and the other, by means of fine wood or wire rods, manipulates the jointed arms, which with emphatic gestures carry on the action of the piece. If working the figure solo is too much for the operator, he is helped by a colleague.

The range of expressions of a rod puppet can be increased by mechanical means. With the aid of special controls the head in particular can be moved and made to bow gracefully and turn from side to side. Puppeteers with technical talent have developed the most divergent methods for producing characteristic or purposefully artificial movements.

Richard Teschner in Vienna achieved an incomparable mastery in the construction and operation of figures of this kind. He was an exponent of the late *Jugendstil* (or 'art nouveau') with a versatility amounting to genius, and in him were combined technical ingenuity and a pronounced sense of the purely artistic. To his first encounter with the Wayang-Golek puppets Teschner owed the decisive stimulus for the mechanical and aesthetic conception of his figures.

The principle of rod puppets, for centuries traditional in the Javanese and Chinese puppet theatre and also in the Asiatic shadow theatre, has since been widely adopted by modern puppeteers, particularly by those in Eastern Europe.

The older type of rod puppet used in the popular Hänneschen-Theater in the Rhineland should be mentioned here. The figures, of a grave clumsiness with dangling legs and only one arm manoeuvrable, are perched on an iron rod, which is inserted into a stout wooden pole the height of a man. They could be belated descendants of those archaic-looking figures previously introduced into mystery plays and processions. They are obviously also the origin of the gigantic figures of the Bread and Puppet Theatre of New York.

A ball at a Paris theatre. About 1841. Anonymous

68 BESTEVA AND BESTEMO
Saarlautern (Germany). About 1920.
From Heinrich Jünger's Kölner Hännes-
chen-Theater.
Wood and textile. Original condition.
Height: 97 cm. (without stick); 270 cm.
(with stick).

Besteva is a bald old tippler. He wears a
frock coat, a red waistcoat, short knee-
breeches and stockings with rings of
colour on them. Hänneschen, who is an
orphan, finds in grumpy Besteva a loyal
companion, always ready for jokes.
Bestemo is a quarrelsome old woman,
with slovenly hair and a gaping mouth.
She has a patterned skirt and blouse, a
white apron and cap. She is Besteva's
wife.
Kasperl in north and south Germany is
a comic figure on his own, but Hänneschen, retaining his natural good sense
in all situations, is surrounded by a whole
range of fantastic characters.
The Hänneschen-Theater, started by
Christoph Winters in 1802, is found in
the Rhineland, in Cologne and Aachen
in particular. The puppets represent types
which have remained unchanged for
generations. Beside Hänneschen and his
girl-friend, Bärbel, they include Tünnes
and Scheel, as well as Besteva and
Bestemo. The figures are placed on tall
iron poles, which in turn are inserted
into long wooden rods reaching to the
ground. The legs hang free. One arm can
be operated.

69 SHEPHERDS
Rome. 1963.
From Maria Signorelli's *Opera
dei Burattini*.
Material and wood.
Height: 58 to 66 cm.

Three Biblical shepherds in faded gar-
ments from *Per la nascita del Redentore*.
Moved hither and thither and illuminated
by a spotlight, the figures come to life
with an extraordinary impressiveness,
thanks to the constantly-changing interplay of the folds of their frequently-
intertwined clothing. Surprisingly graphic
effects and the strongest theatrical im-
pression are achieved with a minimum of
material outlay.

70 FRÄULEIN MUTTER
Vienna. 1913.
Richard Teschner (1879–1948).
Wood and textile.
Height: 40 cm.
A young girl, the tragic chief character
in *Nachtstück*, which conjures up a demonic fairy-tale world.
Teschner's prediliction for the fragile and
unreal, for allegory and metaphor, does
justice to the play, with delicate, graceful rod figures for which he found the
ideal pattern in the Javanese puppet
theatre.

71 FAUN AND NYMPH
Colour plate VIII
Vienna. 1914.
Richard Teschner (1879–1948).
Wood, with some textile.
Height: 45 cm.
Two stark figures, from an erotic piece.
The arms and hands are operated by
long thin sticks; the head — and in the
case of the nymph the body as well — is
controlled by a complicated system of
strings placed inside the supporting rod.

72 MADAME KROCKET
Moscow. 1958.
From the State Puppet Theatre, directed
by Sergei Obraztsov.
Wood and textile.
Height: 80 cm.
A worldly puppet by Boris Tuslukov for
his play, *Mine, mine alone*. With her
audacious décolletage and the snakelike
movements of her arms, she parodies a
vamp.

73 KING
Berlin/Radebeul. 1964.
By Carl Schröder (born 1904).
Wood and textile.
Height: 56 cm.
The avaricious and hardhearted king
from the film version of the fairy story
by the Brothers Grimm, *The Devil with
the Three Golden Hairs*.
Carl Schröder's original and farcical figures are genuinely descended from the
Baroque theatre. His grotesque creations
belong to the world of Jacques Callot.
As a master of hand puppetry and rod
puppetry, an inventive film producer and
a theatre director, Schröder, who works
in the German Democratic Republic, is
widely esteemed.

Mechanical Figures

There have been automatically-operated figures, sometimes so clever that the effects seem almost miraculous, anticipating the idea of robots, ever since the self-propelled dove which the mechanic, Archytas of Tarentum, is supposed to have invented in the year of 390 B.C. Goethe marvelled at Jacques de Vaucanson's artificial duck that waddled and cackled, ate grain, drank water and, after a period for digestion, relieved itself. Heron of Alexandria's automata dispensed wine and milk, and at the Musée d'Histoire at Neuchâtel (Switzerland) are the mechanical human figures of Jacquet-Droz, father and son—Charles the Writer, Henry the Artist and Marianne the Pianist, whose bosom rises and falls as she plays.

Many of the technical devices, regarded now as commonplace at modern production centres, were the outcome of a clever idea of a 'Homo Ludens'—and often the ingenious mind in question was that of a showman who had to develop extraordinary objects to earn the applause of fairground crowds. Many of them became famous for their inventions. For example, princes and emperors expressed a wish to see the automata, Androides and Metamorphoses of Christian Tschuggmall, of Tyrol. The fascination of these figures was not due solely to the amazing naturalness of their movements or the excellence of their mimicry. There was also the way their maker conversed with his creations, with the effect of almost complete animation, and the manner in which he drove them on to their achievements by exhortation, reprimand and praise.

Master-craftsmen, such as Tschuggmall and Matthias Tendler from Styria, thus won legendary reputations through their skill in so coordinating the mechanical resources of their figures that these automatic actors could perform whole episodes while preserving the quaintest air of seriousness.

The princely collections of marvels of the sixteenth century and the travelling displays of mechanical figures alike indicated a propensity for technical experiment and a partiality for the extraordinary.

At the same time, but less important, was the 'Theatrum Mundi', which became significant about 1700 as a kind of epilogue (or after-piece) in the travelling theatres, though it must have existed long before that date. It consisted of a magnificently illuminated stage setting, populated by great quantities of figures of cardboard or tin, fixed on runners on which they could be propelled across the stage in one direction or another. By means of a system of wheels and the use of simple but ingenious machinery, the figures were made to move in a most life-like manner. There might be, for example, a band marching in step or a gondola gliding by under the rhythmic strokes of its oars.

The Theatrum Mundi showed its spectators living pictures—such as the Gulf of Naples, in all its foreign colour and variety, or at night by the light of the full moon, rich with atmosphere. With appropriate musical accompaniment and suitable lighting effects, it supplied sentimental edification, and also knowledge of the world and what was going on in it. It also helped to illustrate and to disseminate information about topical events. Well into the present century it was customary for the Theatrum Mundi to be the final item in the programmes of the popular marionette theatres.

To fill in the intervals between scenes the showmen introduced the so-called 'Metamorphoses'. These were flat cardboard trick figures on strings, hinged and jointed, consisting of several sections, which could be instantly drawn up or let down so that in a flash they changed from one subject to another. The Metamorphoses often had the purpose, sometimes humorous but more generally moral, of unmasking dubious characters. Magic lanterns with their inexhaustible possibilities of optical illusion were used to dazzle the credulous audience with similar transformations.

Magical surprises, reserved as a rule for the final item, could be produced by a projection apparatus with so-called 'Chromatropes'. These were glass slides, painted with geometric ornaments, superimposed on one another and encased in wooden frames. Through handles and levers they could be moved in opposing directions, resulting in a fantastic and kaleidoscopic interplay of colour. They made it possible for even the most humble of travelling companies to offer something of the glitter and enchantment of the romantic theatre and its fairy and magic plays, with the aid of the magic lantern.

Mechanical
Figures

74 FEMALE GYMNAST
Tyrol. Between 1820 and 1830.
From Tschuggmall's Mechanisches Kunsttheater (Mechanical Theatre of Artifice).
Wood, metal and textile.
The mechanism has been damaged.
Height (with extended arms): 56 cm.
With the aid of a mechanism which extends and contracts the figure, the gymnast performs various exercises on the horizontal bar.

Christian Josef Tschuggmall (born 1785 at Wenns, in the Pitz Valley; died 1855 at Michelstadt, Hesse) was a turner and soapboiler at Vahrn, near Brixen. Later he received a commission to construct so-called automata from the Prince Archbishop Count Lodron, for whom he had repaired a watch that no watchmaker could put right. This uncommon man, a technical genius who did not learn to read or write till he was twenty, was responsible for a number of trick figures. They were evolved after years of experiment, and were greatly admired, not only in his native Alpine land but also on his journeys through Poland and Russia. Tschuggmall overcame the very great technical difficulties arising from the construction of his figures and, like all showmen, he maintained the strictest secrecy about them.

From a cut-out sheet of acrobats or street entertainers.
Published by Prepols, of Turnhout, Belgium

75 CIRCUS TURN
Tyrol. About 1828.
From Tschuggmall's Mechanisches Kunsttheater.
Wood and textile.
The mechanism is badly damaged.
Height: 60, 54, 48 cm.
The figures, set up in roundabout-style with a spindle hidden behind their bodies and with the help of strings which are pulled, can execute a complete programme of circus tricks.

76 A DRINKER
Tyrol. About 1828.
From Tschuggmall's Mechanisches Kunsttheater.
Wood and metal. Unclothed figure.
Height: 63 cm; with mechanism, 97 cm.
The bloated face, together with the glass and bottle held ready in the hand, are typical of a confirmed drinker.
If the apparatus beneath the feet, made of levers, a crank and a vertical spindle reaching up into the body, is worked in the right order, the man fills a wine glass and raises it pleasurably to his open mouth, at the same time rolling his eyes. The fluid in the glass flows into a holder, concealed in the chest.

77 WORKING PARTS FOR A MECHANICAL FIGURE
Maker unknown. First half of the nineteenth century.
Brass.
Height: 14 cm.
Clockwork sets in motion the feet and also, eccentrically, the arms (missing) of

the figure, which is so arranged that it hides the mechanism.

78 CROCODILE
Saxony. First half of the nineteenth century.
From the Ritscher Marionette Theatre.
The figure is made of tin, and its substructure of wood and iron.
Length: 105 cm.
The mouth and legs of the crocodile are set in motion by means of a wheel. Figures of this kind were among the attractions of the Theatrum Mundi. In the manner of a news-reel, they were a spectacular addition to the programme of the popular travelling marionette theatres.

79 BEAR
Saxony. First half of the nineteenth century.
From the Ritscher Marionette Theatre.
The figure is made of tin, and the substructure of wood and iron.
Height: 25 cm.
From a Theatrum Mundi. The bear walks naturally and opens its mouth at every step.

80 MUSICIANS

Saxony. Nineteenth century.
From Heinrich Apel's Dresden Marionette Theatre.
Made of cardboard (painted both sides), wood and wire.
Height: 26 to 30 cm.
A brass band marches in step. From a Theatrum Mundi set-piece representing the Dresdener Vogelwiese (fair). In all there are about fifty pieces, including a big wheel, swing-boats, a shooting range and caravans with a menagerie. Some of them were burnt during the war.

81 THE CONQUEST OF ALGIERS

Saxony. About 1850.
A poster for W. Bonneschki's Mechanisches Kunsttheater.
It shows a picture, stretching right across the paper, of the bombardment of Algiers (1830).

Lithograph.
Measurements: 43.5 by 35.5 cm.
The programme of the performance reads: "First Part: The Conquest of Algiers. Second Part: Mechanical Ballet, with a Number of Dances and Metamorphoses. The latter will transform themselves with Surprising Velocity into Various Objects. In the Evenings, instead of the Ballet, there will be Brilliant Fireworks, in the course of which a Selection of Churches, Palaces and Important Buildings, and also Vases and other Items will be displayed, according to the latest methods, in the midst of Bright Fire."

82/83 MAGIC LANTERN

Colour plates VI and VII
Painted glass, in wooden frames.
Size: 12 by 22 cm.
Two circular glass discs, painted and with circular ornaments, are placed on top of

"Ombres Chinoises". Published by the firm of Gangel, of Metz

each other and revolved in opposite directions, producing a kaleidoscopic effect. This speciality was a highlight of the programme. Chromatropes (magic lanterns) were used to illuminate artificial water displays or to project a galaxy of colours on to the undulating white dress of the Serpentine Dancer.

84 GIRL WITH BASKET AND THEATRE (Automaton)
Swiss. About 1860.
The doll's head by Jumeau (Paris). The musical box probably from Geneva. This is an automaton from Neuchâtel.
Size: 78 by 45 by 40 cm.
The standing girl has a wine-red dress and a straw hat on her long, blonde hair. In her right hand she holds a basket and in her left a puppet theatre.
She nods her head in greeting and moves her right hand, at which the lid of the basket is raised. In the basket is a kitten, which rubs its ears. The lid closes, and the doll repeats her greeting. Next the theatre curtain rises. A trapeze artiste appears and performs briefly, whereupon the curtain falls, and the figure once more nods its head. The whole routine is then gone through again, to a musical accompaniment.

85 A MUSICAL NEGRO (Automaton)
Swiss. About 1850.
The head is of papier-mâché, with hands of lead; the mechanism and musical box are Swiss in origin.
Size: 72 by 30 by 30 cm.
The black dandy wears a red tail coat, with a yellow waistcoat, a lace stock and lace cuffs, tight black trousers and a top hat. He stands on a red velvet pedestal, playing a banjo with his right hand. He moves his head to and fro, raises and drops his eyelids and opens and shuts his mouth as if singing a sentimental ditty with a sonorous musical accompaniment.

86 CLOWN AND DONKEY
Germany. Nineteenth century.
The clown's head is of papier-mâché. The donkey is made of wood, with a lamb's skin glued on.
Size: 41 by 26 by 29 cm.
The clown has a red fool's cap, a silk jacket with rose-coloured and lilac sleeves and blue and red trousers. He raises, lowers and moves his head, opens and shuts his mouth. With a baton he conducts the donkey which, sitting on a kitchen stool, turns its head and brays. The musical box, of a considerably later date, plays the Wedding March from *Lohengrin*.

87 a and b. A PEDLAR (A folding Metamorphose or trick figure)
Saxony. First half of the nineteenth century.
From Heinrich Apel's Dresden Marionette Theatre.
Made of cardboard, painted.
Height: 66 cm.
This flat figure, supposedly a pedlar, changes into a pig, apparently so as to be unmasked as a rogue and a cheat. A quick pull on a string with the operator simultaneously stamping his foot brings about this amazing transformation. Presentations of this sort, regarded in many cases as a moral denunciation of human vices, were popular as interludes or to finish a performance.

Imp. lith. Pinot & Sagaire Edit.ª a Épinal   Déposé.

97   Pantins (Jumping Jacks)
Épinal, 1870—80
Published by Pinot and Sagaire
(colour plate IX)

134 Ravana
South Indian shadow figure, 19th century
(colour plate X)

135 Red Prince
South Indian shadow figure, 19th century
(colour plate XI)

102   A woman puppeteer
By a Japanese panorama artist, 1688
(colour plate XII)

European Shadow Puppetry

Johann Kaspar Lavater, the Swiss pastor and author of the book *Physiognomische Fragmente*, wrote in praise of the shadow picture that it reproduces the character and soul of man in the most honest and incorruptible manner and that no other art could reach its truth.

With its witty simplicity, its plasticity, perspective and corporality, the shadow theatre, like silhouettes, enjoyed great popularity in the eighteenth and nineteenth centuries.

Just as the age of enlightenment and the Biedermeier period contrast with the romantic spirit, so the bourgeois taste for silhouette-cutting, terminated by the advent of photography, differs from the imaginative poetry of the shadow theatre, which has never cut itself off from its mythological roots.

The term *ombres chinoises* applied to the shadow theatre, points to the fashionable rococo partiality for *chinoiserie* rather than to China as the country of origin of shadow puppetry. It can just as easily have been brought by sea to Europe from Java, Siam or India. There is also much in favour of the theory that the shadow theatre came via Turkey, where it was in evidence in the sixteenth century, according to travellers' reports, or via North Africa to Italy, whence it spread to Germany, France and England.

It was Dominique Séraphin who elevated it to an art, freed from the taint of trickery. His theatre in the Palais Royal, from 1784 to 1856, was one of the sights of Paris, and its tradition was carried on in the 1880s and up to the turn of the century at the 'Chat Noir' artists' cabaret, founded by Rodolphe Salis.

Cool and enigmatic, shadow puppetry, with all its magical and dreamlike powers, was not without effect on the German romantic movement.

Rediscovering and resuscitating the essence of Justinus Kerner's tales, *Reiseschatten (Travelling Shadows)* and *Der Totengräber von Feldberg (The Gravedigger of Feldberg)*, Alexander von Bernus and his Munich friends, writers and artists, in 1906 founded the Schwabinger Schattenspiele (Schwabing Shadow Theatre) which flourished for a short time. That it lasted less than three years was due to the lack of interest on the part of the public, which gained little real pleasure from the pseudo-romantic happenings in black and white on the stage, especially since the words were delivered, rhythmically or in chant, in the esoteric style of recitation of the adherents of Stefan George.

The cinema's screen and not that of the shadow theatre henceforward was to captivate the masses. Shortly after World War I, Lotte Reiniger's experiment of integrating the shadow theatre into the then young medium of the film, so that all the optical effects of movement could be developed without literary restrictions, met with considerably longer-lasting success, even if that success was by no means revolutionary. With her silhouette-film fairy stories Madame Reiniger, like Ferdinand Diehl, prepared the way for artistic puppet films, among whose greatest creators are Carl Schröder and Jiří Trnka.

88 HERMIT
Munich. End of the nineteenth century.
From *Meggendorfers bewegliche Schattenbilder. II. Vorstellung* (Meggendorfer's Animated Shadow Pictures. IInd. Series).
Published by Braun und Schneider, Munich.
Paper and cardboard; wire springs.
Size: 27 by 28.5 cm.
The transformation picture-books of Lothar Meggendorfer (1847–1925) provide entertainment through a lighthearted combination of shadow pictures and mechanical figures.
From the "Directions for Use:" "This book offers shadow pictures / Which are not difficult to move / And there's a maxim for each. / Any child can understand them easily. / Note carefully — Whoever looks at them / Should be sure that each page is lit up. / Hold them before a window, by day, / And against a light, by night. / Not too far away, and not too close / So that you may see the shadows distinctly. / Do not tug at the strips (of paper) / If the picture is not vertical."
Explanation of the picture shown here:
"The hermit in the forest glade
Lives happily on his own,

And yet all the time
He never lacks for company.
There's many a woodland creature
That knows him well.
Even the proud stag comes to him
And eats out of his hand —
The stag, that otherwise runs from man,
And is seen only from afar.
For he does not question that the hermit
Is a friend of nature indeed!"

89 ARISTOCRAT AND CITIZENESS
France. About 1800.
In the style of Dominique Séraphin (1747–1800).
Sheet zinc and wire.
Height: 50 and 40 cm. (with operating sticks).
From the "Ombres Chinoises" there were evolved shadow figures notable for their comic movements. The creator of this art form, very popular in the age of the silhouette, was Dominique Séraphin François, known as Séraphin. Around 1784 he established a theatre in the Palais Royal, which a century later gave Rodolphe Salis the idea of setting up the Parisian shadow theatre, the Chat Noir. The latter was to become famous, with such artists as Rivière, Caran d'Ache and Willette.

90 WRESTLERS

Berlin. 1962.

The Class of Prof. Herta Schönewolf (Peter Ackermann) at the West Berlin Hochschule für bildende Künste (College of Art and Design).

Ultraphan and metal.

Black drawing ink.

Height: 60 and 50 cm.

"Der Schöne," the handsome one, an athlete equipped with movable biceps, is defeated in a shadow-show parody of wrestling by scraggy "Dreijährigen," the three-year-old, a hinged figure which can make itself large or small at will.

91 DINARSADE

Berlin. 1923.

By Lotte Reiniger (born 1899 in Berlin, she now lives in London).

An animated silhouette, from the shadow film, *Prince Achmed*.

Cardboard.

Height: 38 cm.

Lotte Reiniger has achieved international fame with her shadow films. She began by cutting out title pictures for Paul Wegener's film, *The Pied Piper of Hamelin*. *The Adventures of Prince Achmed* and its successors, *Dr. Dolittle* (1927), *Harlequin* (1931), *Carmen* (1933) and *Papageno* (1935), are considered today to be classic puppet films.

92 TITANIA

Prague. 1965.

By Jiří Trnka (born 1912; died 1969).

A design for the puppet film, based on Shakespeare's *A Midsummer Night's Dream*.

Pencil drawing, signed and dated.

Size: 43 by 27 cm.

A girl in a graceful attitude bedecked with flowers.

Jiří Trnka, the well-known illustrator of books (principally of fairy stories and

"Chinesische Schimmen". Published by Erve Wijsmuller, of Amsterdam

legends), made a great name for himself with his puppet films, *The Emperor's Nightingale* (after Andersen), *A Midsummer Night's Dream, The Good Soldier Schweik, The Song of the Prairie* (a burlesque of the American "Western"), *Prince Bajaja, The Song of the Double-Bass* (adapted from a story by Chekhov), *The Czech Year* and *Old Czech Sagas.*

93   BLAZING FLAMES
Munich. 1926.
By Ferdinand Diehl (born 1901).

Drawing for a scissor-cut film.
Pen-and-ink sketch (section).
Total size: 303 by 50 cm.
Five of eight phases of the finish of a movement.

Ferdinand Diehl, owner of the Diehl Film Company founded in 1929, originated the television hedgehog, Mecki, and has produced countless entertainment, instructional and publicity films. He has made important contributions in the puppet-film field.

The Paper Theatre

The paper theatre is a child of the romantic age. A charming symbol of the sense of family, to which many writers have paid their respects, it was to be found until recent times in every middle-class home.

A heap of cut-out sheets, a pair of scissors, paste and some constructional ability were all that were needed for making a paper theatre, with a few voices and hands to animate its characters. Its basic idea was contained in the old peep-show dioramas, in whose deep, gradated interiors Martin Engelbrecht of Augsburg showed in scenic form religious events and mythological and historical pictures.

It was the paper theatre which imbued the filigree magnificence of such motionless groups and characters with an illusion of life. Since it has moveable figures, which can be slid here and there by means of wires and sticks or even by magnets, the paper theatre is counted among the many forms of puppetry. Fundamentally it is closely associated with the 'live' theatre which, in complete contrast to the intentions of puppetry, it seeks to imitate as closely and with as much authenticity as possible.

The terms 'Toy Theatre' or 'Juvenile Drama' quite wrongly restrict the circle of its enthusiasts to children and young people. In fact it reflects the insatiable delight in plays and entertainments that possessed old and young alike and every class of society after the Napoleonic wars. People were not content to crowd the playhouses and to cover their walls with portraits of favourite performers. To the worship of their adored idols there was added the need to play and act themselves.

Two special factors contributed to the extraordinary popularity of the paper theatre in the nineteenth century. One was the democratization (Verbürgerlichung) of the theatre during the romantic period. The other was the spread of lithography, a cheap printing process, which encouraged the popular colour-print publishers, then springing up all over Europe, to undertake the mass production of paper theatres.

How great the demand was for such products is illustrated by the well-known German collector, Walter Röhler, who stated that, after the immense success of *Der Freischütz* at its first performance in Berlin in 1823, no fewer than sixteen firms issued twenty-five different sets of sheets of characters for Carl Maria von Weber's opera.

The history of a great theatrical century is mirrored, and interesting information about the sociology of public taste is supplied, in the wares of such publishers as Gustav Kuhn and Oehmigke & Riemschneider, both of Neu-Ruppin near Berlin, Scholz of Mainz, Schreiber of Esslingen, Wenzel/Burckhardt of Weissenburg in Alsace, Pellerin of Épinal, Trentsensky of Vienna, and Jakobsen of Stockholm, to mention only a few of the more important firms.

Differing from the Continental paper theatres, the English 'Penny Plain' and 'Twopence Coloured' cut-out sheets were engraved and were considerably smaller in size, with the appellation 'Toy Theatre'.

'Juvenile Drama', like the German paper theatre, reaches back into the eighteenth century, but its heyday was the Victorian age. It achieved great popularity in 1810 when William West in London decided to supply books of words with his sheets of scenes and characters. The best known English publishers were the Webbs, J. Redington, the Skelts and, above all, Benjamin Pollock. They flooded the island, and many other countries as well, with their delightful toylike productions and supplied innumerable families with the means for a domestic hobby, which is still in vogue and for which reprints continue to be made.

94 A PARK
Part of a toy-theatre sheet.
Mainz. Second half of the nineteenth century.
Published by Josef Scholz.
Coloured lithograph.
Size: 33.5 by 41 cm.
Three of six side wings for a park setting. The middle one shows a vase with snakes and agave plants. Those on the left and right have fountains gushing from dolphins' mouths.
The firm of Josef Scholz, founded in 1793, began to turn out toy-theatre sheets when lithographic printing became widespread in Germany in about 1830. The multiplicity of sheets with the same design is explained by the fact that the lithographic stones were constantly being ground down, and the same theme, more or less varying in form, was redrawn each time. See Walter Röhler's book on the paper theatre: *Grosse Liebe zu kleinen Theatern* (Hamburg, 1963).

95 TOM THUMB
Part of a sheet of characters.
Weissenburg (Alsace). About 1880.
Printed and published by C. Burckhardts Nachfolger (C. Burckhardt's Successors) No. 1614.
Coloured lithograph.
Size: 32.5 by 41.5 cm.
Tom Thumb, Alimondate and the Man-eater are naïve, brightly-coloured figures, actors in the paper theatre, with the degree of touching and frightening childishness still called for by lovers of the Bechstein fairy tale.
The firm of Burckhardts Nachf. of Weis-

The Paper Theatre

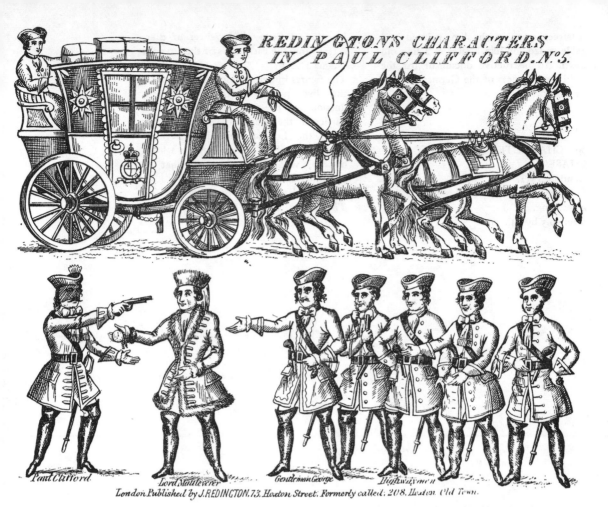

Sheet of characters for the English toy-theatre play, "Paul Clifford". Published by J. Redington

senburg, which entered the then flourishing picture-sheet market in 1860, took over from the Alsace publishing business of F. C. Wenzel, of Wissembourg and Paris.

96 "FOND DE CAMPAGNE" (Backcloth)
Épinal. About 1860.
Published by Pellerin & Cie., Imagerie d'Épinal. No. 1586.
Coloured lithograph.
Size: 39 by 49 cm.
This scene, in the manner of the Old Netherlands "World Landscapes", combines a castle, a bay, a village and a port, suitable for a variety of pieces.
The Imagerie Pellerin, the most important of the French popular print publishers, started producing paper theatres in 1820.

97 PANTINS (Jumping Jacks)
Colour plate IX
Épinal. Between 1870 and 1880.
Published by Pinot & Sagaire (Nouvelle Imagerie d'Épinal) No. 404.
Coloured lithograph.
Size: 24.5 by 39 cm.
Cut-out sheets, with dissected figures: "Titi, Danseur et Danseuse espagnols, Mousquetaire, Bobèche, Ménétrier." The separate parts, pasted on cardboard and cut out and then assembled and linked together at the joints, are worked as jumping jacks when a cord is pulled.

98 TOWN BACKCLOTH
Mainz. About 1840.
Published by Josef Scholz.
Coloured lithograph.
Size: 33 by 43 cm.

55

A street scene, with slim, painted and gable-ended toy-like houses in a fine old town. An instructive document for the architectural ideas of the German romantic period.

99 CHARACTERS IN "CHEVY CHASE"
London. 1832.
Published by Orlando Hodgson
Engraving.
Size: 19.5 by 24.2 cm.

Uncoloured Penny Plain sheet of characters, from the early days of the Juvenile Drama.

The figures imitate in looks and attitudes the "live" players of the original production and preserve the memory of a particular theatrical experience. It was when the London publisher, William West, decided in 1810 to supply a book of words with his cut-out sheets that the Juvenile Drama was born.

See *The History of the English Toy Theatre* by George Speaight (London, 1969).

1 Georg Emanuel Opiz
Kasperltheater, 1805
Gouache

2   William Hogarth
Southwark Fair, 1733
Engraving

3   H. C. Bryard
Punch-Theatre
Oil painting on canvas

4   Giovanni Dura
"Marionnettes à la planchette", 1851
Coloured lithograph

5   Francesco Magiotto
I Burattini, circa 1800
Engraving

6 Louis Marie Lanté
"Paris, Bonne d'Enfant", circa 1820
Coloured engraving

7 Jacques Isidor Grandville
Political caricature
Coloured lithograph

8 Paul Gavarni
Illusionist, circa 1830
Pen and ink sketch

9 Honoré Daumier
Political satire
Lithograph

10   Charles Antoine Coypel
Don Quixote attacking a
marionette theatre, circa 1730
Engraving

11   Richard Teschner
Marionettedrama, 1904
Oil painting on canvas

12   Ferdinand Georg Waldmüller
Childish pleasure, circa 1850
Lithograph

13   The Monogrammatist "FS"
Potato Theatre, circa 1850
Lithograph on a plate

14   Showman's Poster
Schichtls Fantoches Fantastiques, 1910
Chromolithograph

15   Joseph Palta
Kasperl as Apollo
Theatre Curtain (stage front curtain),
circa 1930
From Kuno Ossberger's marionette
theatre, Munich

16   Girl of the Biedermeier Period
Hand puppet, circa 1860
Papa Schmid, Munich

17   Dame à la mode
Hand puppet, circa 1860
Papa Schmid, Munich

18

20

21

19

18   Kasperl
Hand puppet, circa 1925
Toni Schmid, Munich

19   Kasper
Hand puppet, circa 1930
Max Jacob, Hohnstein

20   Guignol
Hand puppet, early 20th century
France

21   Punch
Hand puppet, end 19th century
William Davis, London

22

23

24

25

26

27

22   Laslo Vitez
Hand puppet, end 19th century
From Henrik Kemény's hand-
puppet theatre, Budapest

25   Gretl
Hand puppet, about 1925
South German

23   Vasilache
Hand puppet, 19th century
Rumania

26   Judy
Hand puppet, end 19th century
England

28   Devil
Hand puppet, end 19th century
France

24   Jan Klaassen
Hand puppet, early 20th century
Holland

27   Katrintje
Hand puppet, early 20th century
Holland

29 Prince
Hand puppet, early 20th century
South German

30 A Smith
Hand puppet, early 20th century
Toni Schmid, Munich

31 Civilian and Soldier
Hand puppet, 19th century
Johann Eisen, Munich

33   A Nobleman
Hand puppet, 1864
Ernesto Tortiroli, Cremona

32   Extendable Man
Hand puppet, circa 1870
Lothar Meggendorfer, Munich

34　Vamp
Hand puppet, 1947
Fred Schneckenburger, Zurich

35　Minister and Gossip
Hand puppets, 1925
Max Pokorny, Munich

36　Maid Servant in
"Don Perlimplin"
Hand puppet, circa 1950
Maria Signorelli, Rome

37   Giuramento di Ginamo and Beatrice
and the deaths of Ruggiero Milone
and Almonte
A poster (details)
End 19th century
From Francesco Sclafani's
Marionette Theatre
Palermo

38   Stage Curtain
End 19th century
From Francesco Sclafani's
Marionette Theatre
Palermo

39 A Devil
19th century
Sicily (probably of Taormina)

40 Giants
19th century
Francesco Sclafani, Palermo

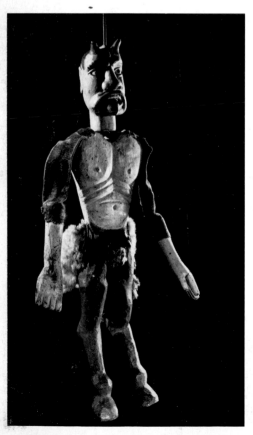

41   The Battle of Roncevalles
     "Opera dei Pupi" (detail), 19th century
     Sicily

42   The Battle of Roncevalles
     "Opera dei Pupi" (full picture)
     Sicily

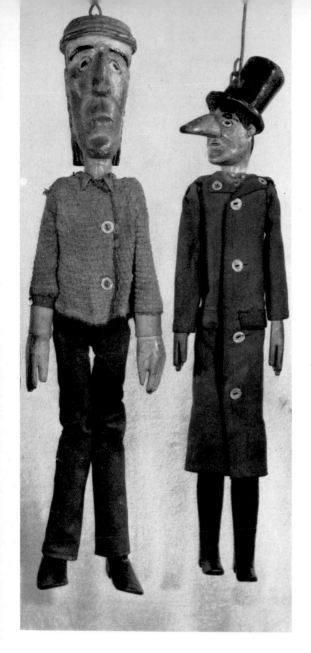

43 Popular Types
19th century
From a Tchantchès theatre, Liége

44 A Burgher
Mid 19th century
From a Toone theatre, Brussels

45 Paladins and Saracen
19th century
From a Tchantchès theatre, Liége

46　A Nobleman
Second half 19th century
Czechoslovakia

47　Kasperl and Two Friends
Second half 19th century
Austria

49　Some of The Best People
End 18th century
England

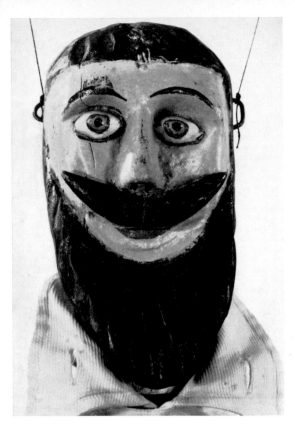

52 Bearded Nobleman
19th century
Johann Jungkunz, Munich

53 A Jolly Girl
Early 20th century
From the Strohbusch travelling
marionette theatre, Halle

54 A Little Devil
19th century
Johann Jungkunz, Bayern

51 Devil
19th century
Johann Jungkunz, Munich

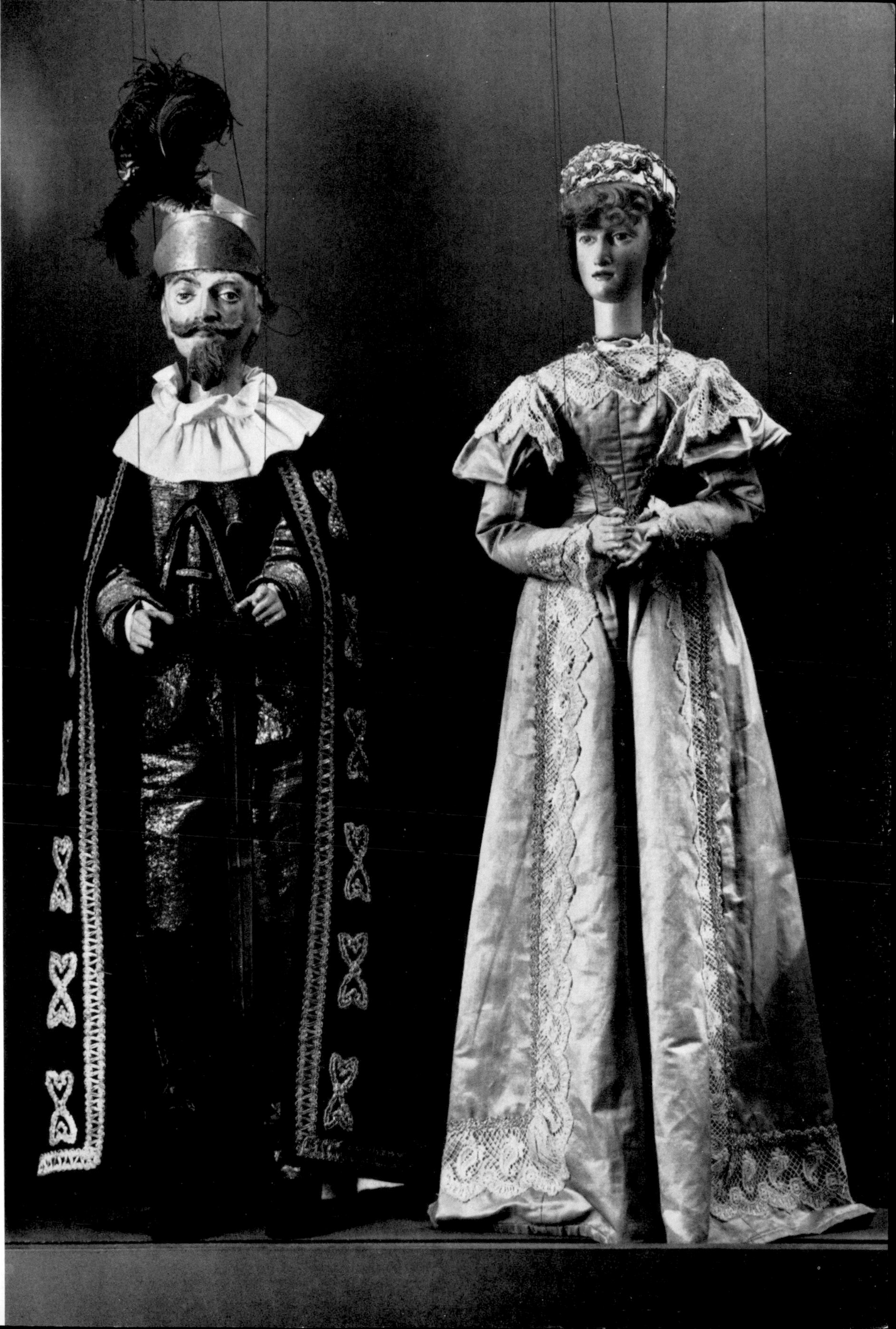

58 Bios and Two Geniuses
1869
Josef Leonhard Schmid, Munich

60 "Goethe Examined"
Circa 1925
Paul Brann, Munich

61 Harlequin and Columbine
1925
Max Pokorny, Munich

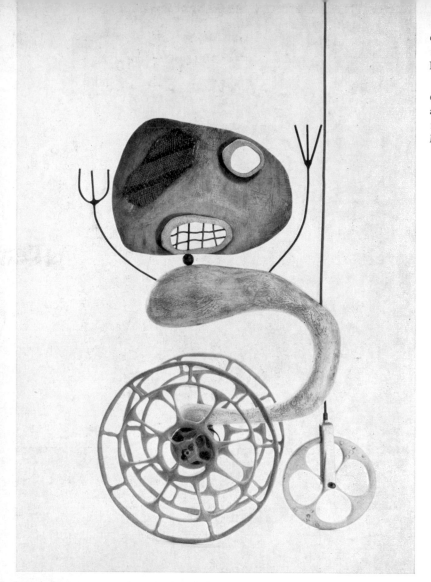

63   Signals in Shadow
1955–9
Harry Kramer, Paris

64   The Rascal Giron
and a Soldier
1964
Michael Meschke, Stockholm

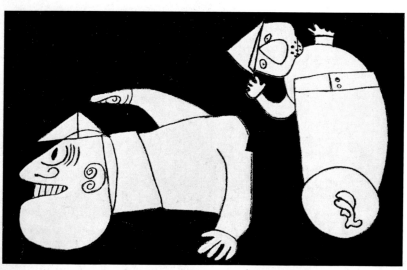

65   Florinde, the Lady without
an Abdomen
1961
Harro Siegel, Brunswick

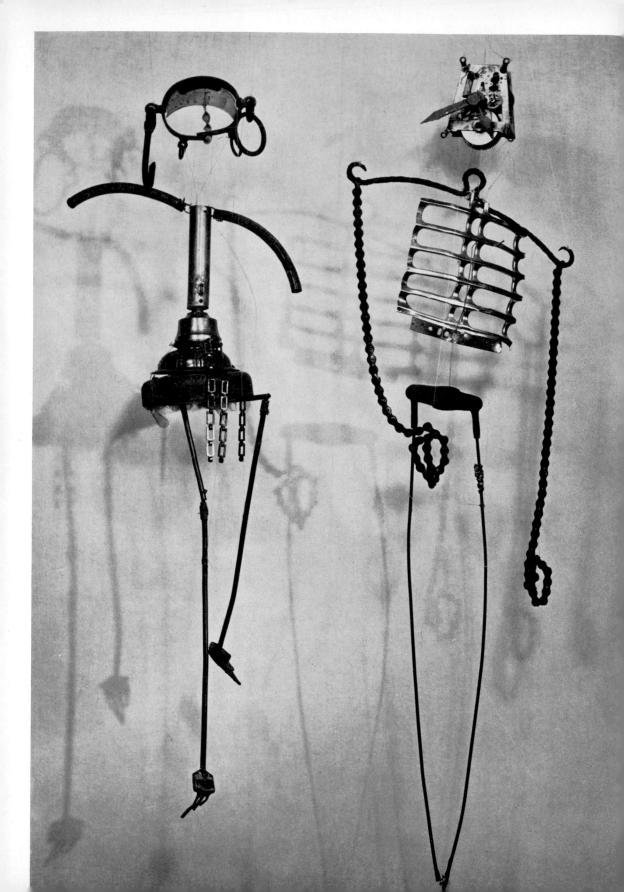

66   Before Midnight
1966
Hochschule für bildende Künste
Berlin

67   Miss Hackit
1936
Walter Oberholzer, Munich

70   Fräulein Mutter
Rod puppet, 1913
Richard Teschner, Vienna

72   Madame Krocket
Rod puppet, 1958
State Puppet Theatre, Moscow

73   King
Rod puppet, 1964
By Carl Schröder, Berlin/Radebeul

68   Besteva and Bestemo
Junger's Hanneschen-Theater
Rod puppets, circa 1920
Heinrich Junger, Saarlautern

69   Shepherds
Rod puppets, 1963
Maria Signorelli, Rome

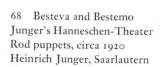

74   Female Gymnast
Mechanical figure, 1820s
Christian Tschuggmall, Tyrol

75   Circus Turn
Mechanical figure, 1820s
Christian Tschuggmall, Tyrol

76   A Drinker
Mechanical figure, 1820s
Christian Tschuggmall, Tyrol

77   Working parts for a Mechanical
figure
First half of 19th century

78   Crocodile
A Theatrum Mundi figure
First half of 19th century
Saxony

79   Bear
From a Theatrum Mundi
First half of 19th century
Saxony

80   Musicians
From a Theatrum Mundi set-piece
19th century
Heinrich Apel, Dresden

81   The Conquest of Algiers
(Mechanisches Kunsttheater)
A poster, circa 1850
Saxony

Mechanisches Kunst-Theater.

Mit hoher obrigkeitlicher Bewilligung

wird Unterzeichnete die Ehre haben Heute zum Erstenmale aufzuführen:

1ᵗᵉ Abtheilung:

Die EROBERUNG von ALGIER.

2ᵗᵉ Abtheilung:

Mechanisches KUNST-BALLET

von mehreren Tänzen u. Metamorphosen. Letztere werden sich mit überraschender Schnelligkeit in verschiedene Gegenstände öffentlich verwandeln.

Anstatt des Ballet, folgt Abends

BRILLANTES FEUERWERK

nach der neuesten Erfindung, wo verschiedene Kirchen u. Paläste u. bedeutende Gebäude, Vasen u. mehrere andere Gegenstände in Brillantfeuer vorgestellt werden.

Preisse der Plätze

Erster Pl. 3 Ngr. — Zweiter Pl. 2 Ngr. — Dritter Pl. 1 Ngr. 3½ Pf.

Der Schauplatz ist

Anfang ist um   Uhr.

W. Bonneschki.

84   Girl with Basket and Theatre
Automaton, circa 1860
Swiss

85   A Musical Negro
Automaton, circa 1850
Swiss

86   Clown and Donkey
Mechanical figure, 19th century
Germany

(a)

(b)

87a and b   A Pedlar
A folding metamorphose or trick figure
First half of 19th century
Heinrich Apel, Dresden

88   Hermit
Animated shadow pictures
End 19th century
Lothar Meggendorfer, Munich

89   Aristocrat and Citizeness
Shadow figures, circa 1800
France

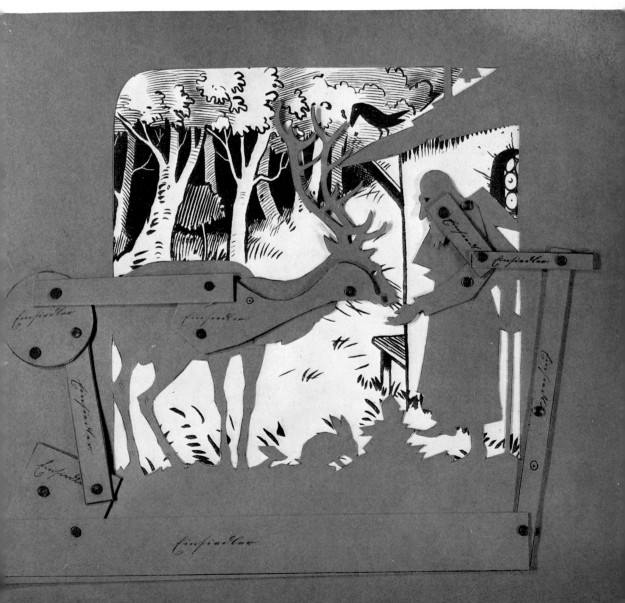

91 Dinarsade
Shadow figure, 1923
Lotte Reiniger, Berlin/London

90 Wrestlers
Shadow figures, 1962
Hochschule für bildende Künste, Berlin

92   Titania
Puppet film design, 1965
Tiří Trnka, Prague

93   Blazing Flames
Drawing for a scissor-cut film, 1926
Ferdinand Diehl, Munich

94   A Park (detail)
Part of a sheet of side wings
Second half of 19th century
Josef Scholz, Mainz

95   Tom Thumb (detail)
Picture-sheet, circa 1880
C. Burckhardts Nachfolger, Weissenburg

96   Fond de Campagne
Paper theatre, circa 1860
Pellerin et Cie., Épinal

98   Town Backcloth
Paper theatre, circa 1840
Josef Scholz, Mainz

Erbtheil von der Base.   Däumling.   Ahmondate.   Menschenfresser.

99   Characters in "Chevy Chase"
Juvenile Drama, 1832
Orlando/Hodgson, London

Non-European Puppetry

The puppet theatre has spread throughout the entire world, and it is also to be found today in places where ethnologically it has no roots of its own.

However much the links with regional traditions may have been relaxed in favour of such an expansion, the avant-garde and those concerned with the revival of puppetry have always remained conscious of the influences latent in the imperishable characters and subject-matter of the popular stage. To mention only a few, Teschner, Puhonny, Obraztsov and latterly Peter Schumann of the Bread and Puppet Theatre of New York have always readily subjected themselves to the strong artistic spirit of the classical puppet theatre.

Socially the most significant and most fascinating form of classical theatre is unquestionably to be found in the Asiatic lands.

Its origins literally go back into legendary obscurity; we have merely to consider the Hindu *Ramayana* and *Mahabharata* epic poems, the main sources of the puppet and shadow plays in all countries from India to Indonesia. In China, puppetry is supposed to have begun during the Han Dynasty (206 B. C. to A. D. 220). In India, where the principal actor in the old Sanskrit theatre was called the *suthradhara* or 'holder of strings', puppetry is presumed to have begun well before the advent of 'live' drama, especially since it is hardly likely that humans would have been permitted to imitate ancestors, heroes and gods.

The most important types, even now by no means completely extinct, such as the Nang Talung of Thailand and the various forms of Wayang in Java and Bali, have preserved intact their ritual cults and mystical character, as if time and fashion had passed them by without leaving a trace.

The old taboo on life-like representations still functions, even in cases where for centuries the performances have been for the purposes of entertainment only. The spectators are not only familiar with the stories in every detail but they also understand down to the slightest nuance the extraordinarily richly articulated language of gesture and mime. The smallest movement has the significance of a metaphor; colours, shapes, ornaments, all have their symbolic meaning, precisely laid down.

The same methods of manipulation as in Europe are used, but shadow, rod and similar figures have become particularly cultivated instruments of the Asiatic puppet theatre.

While shadow puppetry, with flat figures of pierced leather or parchment dyed in many hues, established itself in widespread centres in China, Indonesia, Thailand, India, Turkey and also in Egypt, the special artistic development of the rod figure was concentrated on the Javanese Wayang-Golek and the Japanese Bunraku theatres.

A mythological bull. Indonesian shadow figure

100 BY AN ENGLISH ARTIST (1799)
Chinese one-man theatre.
Aquatint.
Size: 36.5 by 25.4 cm.
The puppeteer performs, standing on a stool enveloped in draperies which hang down to his feet. He carries his hand-puppet theatre on his shoulders.

101 BY AN ENGLISH ARTIST (1814)
Chinese street theatre.
Aquatint.
Size: 25.5 by 16.5 cm.
Operated by an amiable pipe-smoking puppeteer, three musicians (mechanical figures), accompanied by a dog, dance gracefully on top of a box which serves as a stage. They are worked by strings.

102 BY A JAPANESE PANORAMA ARTIST, Genroku style (1688)
Colour plate XII
A woman puppeteer.
Kakemono Sekkei.
Indian ink and body colour.
Size: 167 by 40 cm.
The puppeteer, a member of a Japanese travelling company, uses both hands to manipulate a rod puppet, which must be earlier than the Bunraku theatre.

103 UTASHIGE (Yedo period)
First half of the nineteenth century.
Bunraku theatre.
Coloured woodcut.
Size: 36.4 by 50 cm.
The picture illustrates the most important type of Japanese puppetry. In the upper part is the stage, measuring some eight to ten metres across; below the audience is seen, taking a most active interest.
The name "Bunraku" goes back to Uemura Bunrakuken, a theatre proprietor at Osaka, who doubled the size of his puppets, hitherto worked by one operator only, in order to approximate them to the "live" actors of the Kabuki Theatre. So that they should not be inferior in mime and expression, the puppets' heads were given moveable eyes and eyebrows and also mouths which opened and shut, while the hands had articulated fingers.

The puppeteer, visible to the public, works the puppet's head and right arm, while his two assistants, muffled in black, work its left arm and its feet. Also present are the speaker (a Joruri singer) and a musician who accompanies the narrative on the three-string Shamisen.

104 NETSUKE (Edo epoch)
Eighteenth/nineteenth centuries.
A puppeteer.
Carved ivory, greatly enlarged.
Height: 4.5 cm.
An itinerant puppeteer exhibits his figures (known as "Kugutsu") to a child. He uses as his stage a pedlar's pack which conceals his hands. It looks as though these are rod puppets.

105 TEMES NEVINBÜR
New Caledonia (Oceania). Beginning of the nineteenth century.
A rod puppet for cult performances.
Clay, plant fibre, wood. Painted in earth tints.
Height: 78 cm.
An imposing figure with outspread arms and powerful fangs. Customary for performances before women, children and the uninitiated.
Geometrical ornamentation in white, orange and black is superimposed on a clay-coloured background. Cult figures of this kind are rare, as they were generally burnt after a performance.

106 BAMBARA
Mali (West Africa). Nineteenth century.
A fairy-story teller's figure.
Wood.
Height: 50 and 51 cm.
The figures have elongated, angular heads and deep-set eyes, in which bits of mirror have been inserted, with metal bands and helmet-like head and brow shields. Their throats end in sticks which thicken to form their chest and are then so secured to the operating rods that they can see-saw as the narrator tells his story. There are other Mali figures worked for ritual performances by strings on the principle of a jumping jack, and also various types of rod puppet.

107 IBIBIO

Nigeria (West Africa). Nineteenth century.
Rod puppet for cult ceremonies.
Wood.
Height: 65 cm.
This male figure, wearing a hat, has prominent painted and plastic tribal marks. The arms, legs and head are moveable. Two rods run vertically through the body. One, the control rod, is rigid, and the other, moving freely, operates the opening and shutting of the mouth.

108 KATHPUTLI

North India. Nineteenth century.
A Rajasthan marionette.
Wood. Original state, with considerable evidence of use.
Height: 55 cm.
The head of a man of rank, with well-cared-for whiskers parted in the middle. The marionette has one string only, which runs from the figure's head to the manipulator's hand and back again to the puppet where it is fastened at the back at belt level. Despite this primitive arrangement, the figure can be operated very animatedly and with much precision.
Most of the plays are about the courtly world of the Moghuls.

109 VIDUSAKA AND A COURTIER

Rajasthan. Nineteenth century.
Wood and textile.
Height: 50 and 47 cm.
Vidusaka, a comparatively small figure with a musical instrument and short trousers and jacket, evidences many traits shared by Kasperl and his European cousins.
At his side is a typical Moghul figure with a long white dress but no legs. The action takes place in front of a palace-like setting, painted on material, with arched arcades resembling the architecture of the Taj Mahal.

110 KONANGI

Ceylon. Present century.
Typical figure from a Cingalese theatre.
Wood and textile.
Height: 85 cm.
A white-bearded buffoon, in a fool's costume of motley tufts with a silk shirt, a flat peaked cap with a tassel and frilling at the hands and feet. The character plays a jester's role in a great variety of pieces.

111 DAYA LAKSHMI

Nepal. 1935.
A solo hand puppet.
Papier-mâché and textile.
Height: 36 cm.
The figure represents a young married woman in Nepalese costume consisting of a sprigged skirt, a black blouse, a red scarf and head and arm ornaments.
Daya Lakshmi is weeping for the long absence of her husband who has gone to Lhasa on business. Her mother exhorts her to present a friendly face to the many men who are paying attention to her, and to dance.

112 SITA, RAMA'S WIFE

Thailand. Probably eighteenth century.
Wood and textile.
Height: 52 cm.
A female rod puppet, of capricious delicacy and noble demeanour, with a white symmetrical face and real black hair. The pagoda-like tips of the high golden crown shake with every movement. The dress and collar are richly trimmed with paillettes and galloons. The traditional rod-puppet show, taken from the stories of the *Ramayana*, died out in the nineteenth century.

113 PRINCELY PERSONAGES

Java. Nineteenth and twentieth centuries.
Wayang-Golek figures.
Wood and textile.
Height: 42 to 70 cm.
These are mythical heroes of the *Mahabharata* legends, among them the unconquered Gatotkatja (with wings on its back) with next to it, on the right, Ardjuna and Judistira, two Pandava brothers. Javanese rod puppetry shares with the probably older shadow puppets the filigree delicacy of silhouettes. This is expressed, in the case of the rounded Wayang-Golek puppets, in the mannered, over-elaborate profiles of their heads as well as in the elegant contours of their slender arms and their batik clothing.

A saddled horse. Indonesian shadow figure

The Wayang-Golek puppet theatre aims at a magical alienation of reality. Its discovery and artistic interpretation by Richard Teschner caused a renewal of rod puppetry, in Europe.

114   JUDISTIRA
West Java. Nineteenth century.
A Wayang-Golek figure.
Wood and batik.
Height: 60 cm.
The senior of the Pandava brothers. Despite human weaknesses he is a symbol of justice. The puppet has fine white features, rolled-up hair knots at its neck and a batik skirt.

115   RAMA
East Java. Nineteenth century.
A Wayang-Kelitik puppet.
Painted wood, with arms made of leather.
Height: 60 cm.
Rama, the chief character of the *Ramayana*, is an incarnation of Vishnu. In accordance with his importance, this figure displays a high degree of formal beauty. The head and gaze are nobly lowered. Rama has a crown (*makuta*), wings on his back (*praba*) and an artistic puffed-out costume, suitable to his regal position, with a dagger (*kris*) and bracelets on his arms and legs.

The Kelitik figures, still to be found only occasionally in Central and East Java, are handled and operated like rod puppets. They approximate, however, to shadow figures because they are in bas-relief.

116   A CELESTIAL GENERAL
China. Eighteenth century.
A rod puppet. Origin unknown.
Wood, textile and papier-mâché.
Height: 58 cm.
A character inspiring fear, the face painted blue, white and red with angry, staring eyes, a towering martial head-dress and a beard which hangs down in several separate strands. The magnificent costume is of red embroidered silk. Rods to control the movements of the puppet are hidden in its sleeves.

117   A FOOLISH OLD MAN
China. First half of the nineteenth century.
Ho Giok Lan hand-puppet theatre. Djakarta.
Wood and textile.

Height: 32 cm.

A figure of macabre jollity and naïveté. The forehead is abnormally high, with the remains of a tuft of hair. The white face resembles that of a clown, and the toothless mouth opens and shuts by means of the hinged chin.

118 A SERVANT
China. First half of the nineteenth century. Ho Giok Lan hand-puppet theatre. Djakarta.

Wood and textile.

Height: 35 cm.

The red colouring on his face, symbolizing manly virtues, is perhaps intended to express the loyalty and honesty required of a servant. The brutality of his features shows him to be a man of lowly position. The monstrous bulging forehead stresses the vulgarity of his appearance and indicates that a character from daily life was observed with unmerciful realism.

Khrut frees Phra Lak. Thai shadow figure

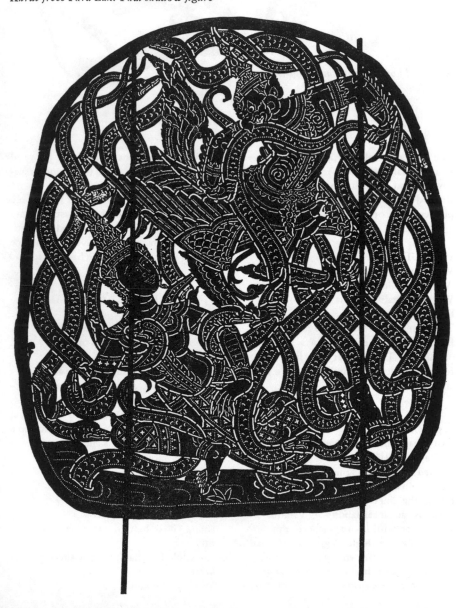

119 THE EMPEROR LI SI BIN
China. First half of the nineteenth
century.
Ho Giok Lan hand-puppet theatre.
Djarkarta.
Wood and textile.
Height: 34 cm.
The fine face conveys magnanimity and
goodness and the splendid fur-edged
dress imperial majesty. The figure has
legs and boots with thick soles.
It is one of a group of ninety-three hand
puppets, now in the possession of the
Munich Collection. They were probably
used for popular pieces, such as *The Pil-
grimage to the West* and *The Three-Em-
peror Time*.

120/121 KIYOHIME (Trick figure)
Japan. About 1965.
From the Takeda Marionette Theatre,
Tokio.
The figure and mechanism are by Kino-
suke and Sennosuke Takeda.
Wood and textile.
Height: 70 cm.
Princess Kiyohime, a charming young
woman in a red flowered kimono, can be
transformed into a terrifying demon by
pulling a single string. Suddenly her teeth
become sawlike, her eyes are distorted
and shine like gold, and there are horns
in her hair.

122 YASHA
Japan. Seventeenth century.
Sekkyo-bushi theatre.
Wood and real hair.
Original state, damaged.
Height: 12 cm.
Kashira (head) of a Medusa-like demon.

This frightening apparition, called Yasha,
was used in the recitations of the Sekkyo-
bushi theatre, whose heyday was in the
sixteenth and seventeenth centuries. It
can still occasionally be found in remote
country areas.
See Gitta Lepsius: *Das heutige japanische
Puppentheater auf dem Lande und seine
Vorgeschichte.* Published by the Gesell-
schaft für Natur- und Völkerkunde Ost-
asiens e. V., Hamburg, 1968. *(The Contemporary Japanese Puppet Theatre in the
Country and its Antecedents,* published by
The Society for Nature and Ethnology
in East Asia, Hamburg, 1968.)

123 SEKKYO-NINGYO
Japan. Seventeenth century.
Sekkyo-bushi theatre.
Wood. Original condition, badly damaged.
Height: 18 cm.
Kashira (head) of a rod puppet, whose
significance is no longer clear; probably
neither demonic nor comic. Despite extensive damage and missing lacquer the
plastic quality of the head can still be
clearly recognized.

124 COURTESAN
Japan. Second half of the nineteenth
century (Meiji period).
Bunraku theatre.
Wood and textile.
Height: 120 cm.
The magnificent embroidered kimono,
with the Obi here knotted in front, shows
this female figure to be a great courtesan. The lavish use of gold embroidery,
partly in relief, denotes her prosperity.
A dragon and a fish are the main themes
of the ornamentation.

Asiatic Shadow Puppetry

The puppet theatre which is found in many forms and in all parts of the world, reaches its highest degree of refinement in Asiatic shadow puppetry. Without forfeiting its deep-rooted popular nature or losing anything of its contact with the public, in streets and market places and even in the remotest villages, the Asiatic shadow theatre achieves an almost esoteric spirituality through the artistic stylization of its figures and the magic ceremonial of its presentation.

From the skins of goats, sheep, donkeys, camels or cattle are produced delicate transparent figures of parchment, scraped thin and coloured, or of roughly-tanned stiff leather, in the latter case looking like out-size scissor cuts. Chiselled and punched out by untiring hands, there emerge from coarse materials noble and horrific forms, lineaments and ornamental designs superbly stamped, which, for all their liveliness and profusion, are invariably simple to the point of abbreviation and disclose a disciplined sense of economy and restraint. Even the exotic baroque of the Wayang-Kulit figures of Java and Bali, which are painted as well as perforated, is characterized by a formal arrangement, controlled down to the slightest detail.

The puppet is not associated with reality in the shadow theatre, whose classical centres have been in Old Siam, Java, the Western Chinese province of Szetschuan and Peking, while also enjoying the greatest popularity, but in each case in distinct styles, in South India, Turkey and Egypt. Shadow puppetry is not concerned, as with marionettes, or hand or rod puppets, with three-dimensional bodies and a spatial stage, but with flat figures moving on a two-dimensional plane which, as a rule, the spectator does not see directly in front of him.

The eye observes only the shadows projected on a white linen or silk

140 Wilmana
Bali, 19th century
Wayang-Purwa shadow figure
(colour plate XIII)

153   Saddled horse
Chinese shadow figure
Early 19th century
(colour plate XIV)

154 Butterfly
Chinese shadow figure
Early 19th century
(colour plate XV)

144   Triple-headed elephant
Thailand, Nang Luong figure,
19th century
(colour plate XVI)

screen. As though coming from nowhere, they float nearer and assume contours and shapes, only to dissolve again and to return to the same nothingness. An atmosphere of strange restlessness and unreality is created by the fluctuating movement to and fro of shadows or coloured forms, which rapidly become tiny while consolidating into material shapes as they approach, but grow into ever larger and more ghostly forms as they retreat, before vanishing like apparitions.

The use of optical and illusionistic aids in shadow puppetry, astonishingly modern in effect, constitutes one of the most interesting chapters in the history of the theatre. At the same time it is the puppet itself, through its filigree beauty, its rare and vivid magic, which enriches the history of non-European art with such an impressive special contribution.

Shadow puppetry recalls—if we think primarily of the Thailand Nang figures of pierced buffalo leather or the elegant Szetschuan figures cut from parchment and coloured—the stained-glass windows, so severe in their magnificence, of Western cathedrals and churches.

At the same time one must be careful not to regard as works of art in their own right objects which fascinate by their bizarre ornamentation. Their true nature, depending on illusion and hallucination, is revealed only in their movements, or to be more precise in the projection of those movements. If the old historic shadow play, inconceivable without the white screen and the effect of light, is regarded as an archaic pre-form of the cinema or even of the modern colour film (entertainment media responsible for its extinction), then the individual figure has merely the significance of a 'still' photograph. But this comparison also is imperfect since such an individual figure, removed from the continuity of the play, is no more than a sort of secret cipher, which anyone not familiar with the religious concepts of the East is unable to understand, and which even scholars can never unravel completely.

When Alexander von Bernus says of the shadow play that it reflects 'in its purest form the dematerialized world of waking dreams', he has in mind the magic area where the threshold between this and the next world is crossed by ghosts and demons, such as the clearly differentiated good and bad characters of the *Ramayana* and the *Mahabharata* legends.

Uncanny shadow play seances, lasting from sunset to sunrise, took place, as they still do occasionally, on feastdays, at weddings, at births and circumcisions, or after a death. If a beautiful legend may be believed, they had their origin in China, where once upon a time an emperor, mourning the death of his favourite wife, summoned at night a shadow puppeteer to conjure up her spirit. But even an approximately precise date for the rise of the Chinese shadow theatre cannot be established. The fact that such eighteenth and nineteenth century figures as survive have a stilted charm and an air of desultory aimlessness could point to their being a late variation of very ancient forms; this theory is supported to a certain extent by the mechanical perfection of the method of operation. Equally, however, the Peking and Szetschuan figures could be of no great age but the result of an adjustment of the Nang and Wayang type to court and fashionable conventions.

Nor can any exact estimates be made as to the age and origin of Siamese and Javanese shadow puppetry, and the same must be said of a scarcely less significant artistic and ritual phenomenon, the Egyptian shadow theatre.

How far the silhouetted figures of the Greek vase paintings influenced the concept of shadow puppetry remains a matter for conjecture. But no one can deny the striking resemblance between the character, always disposed to obscene jokes, which has the title role in the Turkish Karagöz plays, and the phallic satyr of antiquity.

It is likely that the roots of the shadow theatre go very far back to remote civilizations. Its figures, fugitive yet tenacious of life, are vital documents of early periods and also of the height of former cultures.

Egypt

The Egyptian shadow theatre can be shown to have been in existence in the thirteenth century. There seems to have been a connection with the Turkish shadow theatre. It is rumoured that Egyptian shadow puppeteers repeatedly visited Turkey in the sixteenth and seventeenth centuries. Despite the historical links, there are considerable differences. Whereas Turkish shadow puppetry is closer to the prosaic reality of the Chinese, the Egyptian figures have an archaic severity, with the purely ornamental outweighing interest in the subject.

Few early Egyptian figures have survived, as almost all were destroyed on the orders of the orthodox Sultan Tschaknak, who caused them to be burnt in the fifteenth century.

125 COPTIC PRIEST
Egypt. Fourteenth century.
Shadow puppet.
Camel skin.
Height: 52 cm.

A walking priestly figure, clad in sacred robes; the severely stylized face is turned toward the spectator. In one hand is a brush for sprinkling holy water; the other, the little finger of which has rings on it, has hold of the beard. The dress has open-work, lattice-type ornamentation and various patterns on sharply-contoured planes. There are traces of transparent coloured membranes. Damaged places have been underlaid with parchment.

The figure was discovered in 1909 by Professor P. Kahle at Menzaleh, in the Nile Delta, together with other mediaeval Egyptian shadow puppets.

Bibliography: Georg Jacob: *Geschichte des Schattentheaters im Morgen- und Abendland (The History of the Shadow Theatre in the East and the West)* Hanover, 1925. Paul Kahle: *Das arabische Schattentheater im mittelalterlichen Ägypten (The Arabian Shadow Theatre in Mediaeval Egypt).* In *Wissenschaftliche Annalen* – Third Year: 12 December, 1954. Published by the Akademie-Verlag. L. Keimer (Cairo): *La figure d'un prêtre copte dans un ancien théâtre d'ombres d'Egypte (The figure of a Coptic priest in an old Egyptian shadow theatre) Cahiers Coptes* – 1956. No. 11.

Turkey

There are very divided opinions as to the age and origin of Turkish shadow puppetry. It is asserted that Karagöz and Hacivad, the two leading characters of the Turkish shadow theatre, existed as real people in the thirteenth century. The grave of Karagöz is supposed to be in a cemetery at Bursa and that of the puppeteer who allegedly invented Karagöz is also said to be known. According to another version, Turkish shadow puppetry derives from that of China, if only because of the transparency of the figures. Camel skin was used, and the performances took place at night, generally in a coffee house, part of which would be separated by a curtain with a rigid frame in the middle across which a white linen sheet was stretched. Behind the screen (perde) the puppeteer by means of rods operated the jointed transparent coloured figures. Each play—and some forty of them are known—begins with a conversation between Karagöz and Hacivad, forming the prelude to the actual plot. That the plays have become very rare, and today only survive hidden away, may in part be due to their strong political and social-critical content, as well as their erotic and obscene nature.

In addition to this very popular form there is, too, the refined variant of the so-called *serail* (seraglio) plays.

Karagöz may still be found in Greece, where he is called Karagiosis.

126—129 POPULAR FIGURES
Turkey. Nineteenth century.
Characters from a Karagöz theatre.
Parchment, in part uncoloured, otherwise red, yellow and green.
Height: 30 to 33 cm.
From left to right: Beberuhi, a dwarf and village idiot, with horn-shaped headdress; Curcunabaz, a grotesque dancer; Zenne, a fine lady; Karagöz (Blackeye), the chief character of this piece, who is led into all sorts of adventures by Hacivad, the village spokesman.

India

In India also there are no clues as to the start of shadow puppetry. The fact that the *Ramayana* and *Mahabharata* Sanskrit epic poems serve as sources for the plays permits certain conclusions as to their age, but authentic chronological indications are lacking.

Tolu Bommalata, the form most in use today in South India, consists of transparent figures about 100 to 180 cm high, which are brightly coloured and striking. Each figure is held in a split rod. Many have sticks to their arms as well. Performances are given on open spaces or in the village street, behind a screen, consisting sometimes just of two saris fixed securely one above the other. The elephant-headed god, Vighneswara, surrounded by animal figures, is hung up in front of the screen and removed before the show starts. The principal of the family troupe speaks a prologue and the play begins. The proceedings are additionally emphasized by music on popular instruments. The performances begin late at night and continue till morning.

130 DEMON (Rakshasa)
Madras (South India).
Nineteenth century.
Tolu Bommalata.
Parchment, strongly coloured.
Height: 120 cm.
Black skin; elegant flower ornaments on the face; spherical eyes; an extended fang in the corner of the mouth; short red trousers. The right foot has been restored.

131 DEMON (Rakshasa)
Madras (South India).
Nineteenth century.
Tolu Bommalata.
Parchment, strongly coloured.
Height: 110 cm.
Shown *en face*. The face and body are black. Spherical eyes; sharp teeth and fangs; red trousers; a band across the chest. The arms and hands are pink, and the feet red.

132 A FEMALE DANCER
Madras (South India).
Nineteenth century.
Tolu Bommalata.
Parchment, strongly coloured.
Height: 104 cm.
A magnificently ornamented maiden with plaited hair. Her face is bright pink and she has a blue jacket, with a red open-work sari. Her feet are bare but they are covered in rings and bracelets.

133 A PERSON OF RANK
Possibly a special form of the Dharmaradja.
Madras (South India).
Nineteenth century.
Tolu Bommalata.
Parchment, strongly coloured.
Height: 125 cm.
A distinguished character with a severe bearing. His face and hands are pink and

his legs red. He has a black flower-patterned coat and a light-coloured turban and scarf.

134 RAVANA
Colour plate X
Madras (South India).
Nineteenth century.
Tolu Bommalata.
Parchment, strongly coloured.
Height: 109 cm.
The King of Lanka in Ceylon. He has ten crowned heads and ten arms, and is the main character in the *Ramayana* epic poem. He wears a splendid and richly ornamented garment of blue and orange and sits, covered in jewels, on a lion throne with his bare feet on gold-braided cushions.

135 RED PRINCE
Colour plate XI
Madras (South India).
Nineteenth century.
Tolu Bommalata.
Parchment, strongly coloured.
Height: 180 cm.
Thought to be Ardjuna, third eldest of the Pandava brothers *(Mahabharata)*. The upper part of the body is bare. There is an excess of decoration. The head and body are red with black trousers with red ornaments. One arm has been replaced.

Indonesia

Indonesian shadow puppetry is known as Wayang (the original term for shadow) or more exactly Wayang-Kulit (kulit means leather). Its existence was reported in the eleventh century. It is to be found in Java and Bali in two iconographic forms. The classical form of Wayang-Kulit, based on very old texts *(lakon)*, principally the Indian heroic *Mahabharata* and *Ramayana* poems and the Ardjuna Sasra Bau cycle, is called Wayang-Purwa. From it have stemmed additional types of Wayang-Kulit, which in their turn influence other groups of sagas. One of the best known variations is that of the Wayang-Gedog, based on the legends of Prince Pandji and the hero Damar Wulan. Later, thanks to princely

initiative, the kulit repertoire in Java was constantly extended. After 1945 more modern forms of Wayang-Kulit, with predominantly political themes, were introduced, and various religious interests have made use of Wayang puppetry.

Wayang-Kulit performances take place at night and go on till break of day. The shadow screen *(kelir)* is set up in a closed area or a roofed-in place. In front of the screen are banana trunks, into which the dalang, who is both puppeteer and sole speaker, sticks the figures. The lighting is supplied by a lamp *(blentjong)* hanging above the dalang. The male spectators, and particularly the guests of honour, sit behind the dalang, where they can directly see the richly painted figures. The rest of the audience see merely the shadows. The seating arrangements are less strict in Bali. Performances are given on special occasions, such as marriages, births, circumcisions, etc., but also to drive out bad spirits or when there is an illness. Special figures are then introduced into the show. The musical accompaniment comes from a Gamelan orchestra, which has its traditional place at the rear of the dalang.

136 ARDJUNA
Jogjakarta (Java). Start of the present century.
Wayang-Purwa puppet.
Parchment, painted.
Height: 46 cm. (without control stick).
A leading character in the *Mahabharata*. Third eldest of the Pandavas, a son of Prabu Pandus and an incarnation of Vishnu, he possesses magic powers and is regarded as a symbol of male heroism. This specimen has a gilded face and body, high knots of hair *(gelung supit urang)* and a princely dress, puffed out like a balloon, on the lower half of the body. It wears no throat ornaments or arm or foot bracelets, and belonged to a court theatre.

137 BATARA KRESNA (Krishna)
Jogjakarta (Java). Start of the present century.
Wayang-Purwa puppet.
Parchment, painted.
Height: 52 cm. (without control stick).

120

Garuda. Indonesian shadow figure

A leading figure in the *Mahabharata*, Krishna is the incarnation of Vishnu and a councillor of the Pandavas. He can transform himself into a giant *(brahala)* and has at his disposal the Tjakra weapon, which is reserved to the incarnations of Vishnu.

The face is black, and the body golden with a dress puffed out like a balloon, a crown *(makuta)* and wings on its back *(praba)*. Copious ornaments. A figure from a court theatre.

138 GUNUNGAN
Bali. Nineteenth century.
Wayang-Purwa puppet.
Parchment, painted.
Height: 54 cm. (without control stick).
A tree of life or heaven. Here it rises out of the lotus and in its towering form serves also as a symbol of the mountain. At the start and finish of a performance, and during intervals in the narration, the gunungan is placed in the centre of the screen. Its other side is often painted red, and it also signifies fire and wind. In both cases it is vigorously moved to and fro.
The Balinese gunungan is rounded at the top, in contrast to the Javanese one which is tapered off. On most of the gunungans there are representations of guards by a door, mythological snakes and a demon's head *(kala)*.

139 BRAHALA
Bali. Nineteenth century.
Wayang-Purwa puppet.

Parchment, painted.
Height: 59 cm. (without control stick).
A blue-tinted giant with several heads and arms, equipped with weapons which include a tjakra (a wheel-shaped projectile).
In Wayang stories only Prabu Kresna, Prince of Dwarawati, and Prabu Ardjuna Sasra, Prince of Maespati, two incarnations of Vishnu, are able to turn themselves into giants of this kind. Batara Kresna assumed this form before the Bratajuda War when he sought in vain to settle the quarrel between the Pandavas and the Korawas.

140 WILMANA
Colour plate XIII
Bali. Nineteenth century.
Wayang-Purwa puppet.
Parchment, very much painted.
Height: 46 cm. (without control stick).
A bird-like creature on which the king from Ceylon, Ravana, also called Dasamuka, rides.
It has the face of a bird of prey, with wings and taloned feet. The body is green and richly ornamented in gold. The wings have greenish-blue and red feathers. The short garment round its waist has a chessboard pattern.

141 PRAHASTA
Solo or Jogjakarta (Java).
Nineteenth century.
Wayang-Purwa puppet.
Parchment, painted.
Height: 84 cm. (without control stick).
A double-eyed giant prince, whose face and body have a golden background, with disks on the forehead and a Garuda clasp in the hair which hangs down. Richly decorated. Only one arm moves. Prahasta is the first minister of Ravana, the giant prince of Lanka, Ceylon.

142 SEMAR
Java. Nineteenth century.
Wayang-Purwa puppet.
Parchment, painted.
Height: 40 cm. (without control stick).
Originally a son of the gods with a pleasing form, Semar was transformed into a monster, with every conceivable deformity of the human body. He was destined

to be the servant of the gods travelling on earth. However repellent his exterior, he has, nevertheless, brains and wit. He usually appears with his sons, Petruk and Gareng, who do not lag behind their father in grotesque disfigurement.

In the evening and at night Semar is seen completely gilded, but as morning approaches he has a white face and a black body.

Thailand and Cambodia

As with Indian shadow puppetry, the Thailand shadow theatre is based on the *Mahabharata* and *Ramayana* Sanskrit epic poems, called in Thailand *Ramakien*.

Shadow puppetry in Thailand is first referred to in 1458 in a law of King Boromatrailokanath.

Apart from ancillary forms, it has two main types. The first, the older one, is Nang Luong, found in the north of the country and known as the royal shadow puppet theatre (Nang Yai); it makes use of large figures, made of incised buffalo hide, which look like pictures. The incorporated figures are not articulated, nor are the individual, separate figures. Some pieces are as much as two metres high. There are also the Nang Talung puppets, with smaller figures, some 50 cm. tall, whose limbs are partially moveable. They take their name from the southern province of Patalung.

Both the Nang Luong and the Nang Talung theatres are invariably shown at night. The screen is slightly tilted. After preliminary ceremonies the actual Nang Luong performance begins. To the music of the Gamelan orchestra and operated from behind the screen, the figures are made to dance rhythmically. A further variation, comparable with the Nang Luong, still survives in Cambodia. A different choreography, by contrast, is required by the Nang Talung puppets, since their limbs must be operated. The technique in this instance is related to that of the Indonesian shadow theatre.

143 SUKHRIP (with four monkeys)
Thailand. Nineteenth century.
Nang Luong (Nang Yai) shadow figure.
Buffalo hide, blackened, with partial red shading.

Height: 180 cm. (without control sticks).
The monkey prince, Sukhrip, urges his army to fight, in an episode from the *Ramayana*. There is a leather binding round the whole.

144 TRIPLE-HEADED ELEPHANT
Colour plate XVI
Thailand. Nineteenth century.
Nang Luong (Nang Yai) shadow figure.
Buffalo hide, transparent parts, blackened and coloured.
Height: 140 cm. (without control sticks).
A demon, transformed into a multi-headed elephant by Inthorachit, who rides it in a subsequent fight against Hanuman. The figure, resembling a picture puzzle with unusual colouring, is leather-edged.

145 VISHNU
Cambodia. Nineteenth century.
Nang figure.
Buffalo hide, partially blackened.
Height: 76 cm.
The god, Vishnu, on his mount, the divine bird, Garuda (Khrut). From the *Ramayana*.

146 MONKEY AND GUINEA FOWL
Cambodia. Nineteenth century.
Nang figure.
Parchment, blackened.
Height: 38 cm.
A little monkey squats on the back of an ornamented guinea fowl.

147 KUMPHAKAN
Thailand. Nineteenth century.
Nang Luong figure.
Buffalo hide, blackened, and red, green and transparent in part.
Height: 140 cm. (without control sticks).
A demon prince, brother of Thotsakan and Ravana and Viceroy of Lanka club in hand, stands on a mythological snake *(naga)*. This single figure, from the *Ramayana*, has no leather edging round it.

China

China is held to be the country of origin of shadow puppetry, and from there it spread to South East Asia. Although textual references occur first in the tenth and eleventh centuries, it can be assumed that the shadow theatre existed in China earlier than then. The performances were partially instructive and partially popular entertainment, but they were seen also at the imperial court. The repertoire consisted of plays of Buddhist or Taoist content, sometimes with burlesques.

Chinese shadow puppetry has two sorts of figures. Those in one category are about 25 cm. high, of parchment made from donkey skin, and are to be found in the vicinity of Peking. The second sort are from the province of Szetschuan. Made from buffalo parchment, they measure 70 to 80 cm.

There is remarkable subtlety in the cutting, the colouring and the mechanism of operating both the small and the large figures. The various parts are joined by thread and are worked by means of a control stick, attached by a swivelled frame to the centre of gravity of the figure. The arms, which are movable, are manipulated by rods. The strength of the lower part of the figure emphasizes the elegance of the body.

A few traditional musical instruments accompany the action. The operators, who are also the speakers, are placed behind a more or less artistically ornamented screen. The original means of illumination, an oil lamp, has been replaced by electric light.

148 SNAKES
Szetschuan. Early nineteenth century.
Chinese shadow figures.
Parchment.
Length: some 150 cm. each.
Black and red snakes breathing flames, with ten and twelve joints in their bodies. They appear in the play *The White Snake* as beautiful demon women.

149 SCORPION
Szetschuan. Early nineteenth century.
Chinese shadow figure.
Parchment.
Height: about 60 cm.
A mythological animal figure. A male

or female scorpion-demon which assumes human shape.

150 TORTOISE
Szetschuan. Early nineteenth century.
Chinese shadow figure.
Parchment.
Height: 25 cm.
A mythological symbol for long life, sexual power and fertility.

151 CLOUD
Szetschuan. Early nineteenth century.
Chinese shadow figure.
Parchment, partially coloured.
Size: some 20 by 60 cm.
A strongly stylized graphic representation of a cloud, implying prosperity. It can also have other meanings, according to its shape.

152 WHITE SNAKE AND BROTHER-IN-LAW
Szetschuan. Early nineteenth century.
Chinese shadow figure.
Parchment, partially coloured.
Height: 70 and 76 cm.
Left: A female demon in human form, known as the White Snake. In travelling costume with hat.
Right: A male figure, called Brother-in-Law. On the chest crane ornamentation; the trousers have a flower pattern.
Both figures belong to the play, *The White Snake*.

153 SADDLED HORSE
Colour plate XIV
Szetschuan. Early nineteenth century.
Chinese shadow figure.
Parchment.
Height: 50 cm.
An elegant black horse with a docked tail. The saddle is ornamented in red, yellow and black and laid on a blue-bordered blanket. The bridle is embellished with tassels and bells. The knee-joints are movable. The use the figure was put to is not known.

154 BUTTERFLY
Colour plate XV
Szetschuan. Early nineteenth century.
Chinese shadow figure.

Parchment.
Height: 44 cm.; Breadth: 69 cm.

An uncommon design in red and black. Spots resembling eyes in several colours on a transparent base. One wing is movable and can be opened. Its use is not known.

155 HOUSE

Peking. Early nineteenth century.
Chinese shadow figure.
Parchment, with red and blue colouring.
Height: 78 cm.
An architectural set-piece, richly ornamented and coloured. From a small-figure shadow theatre, Pekinese in character.

Next three pages:

103 Utashige
Bunraku Theatre
First half of 19th century
Coloured woodcut

104 Netsuke
A puppeteer, 18th/19th century

100 By an English Artist
Chinese one-man theatre, 1799
Aquatint

101 By an English Artist
Chinese street theatre, 1814
Aquatint

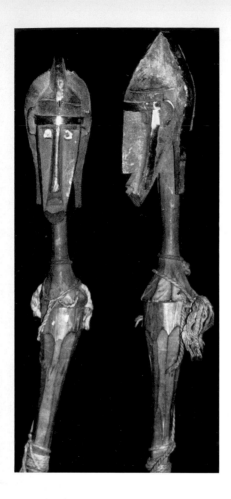

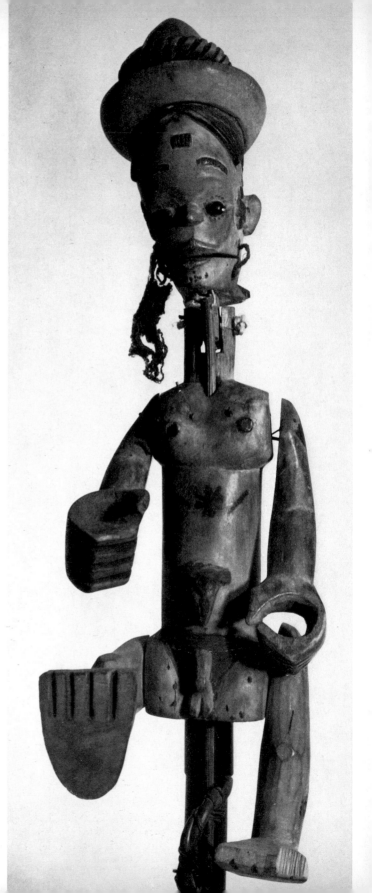

106   Bambara
Rod puppet, 19th century
Mali (West Africa)

107   Ibibio
Rod puppet, 19th century
Nigeria (West Africa)

108   Kathputli
A Rajasthan marionette, 19th century
North India
(Opposite page)

Previous page:

105   Temes Nevinbür
Rod puppet, early 20th century
New Caledonia (Oceania)

109   Vidusaka and a Courtier
A Rajasthan marionette, 19th century
North India

110   Konangi
20th century
Ceylon

111   Daya Lakshmi
Hand puppet, 1935
Nepal

112 Sita, Rama's wife
Rod puppet, probably 18th century
Thailand

113 Princely Personages
Wayang-Golek figures, 19th/20th century
Java

114 Judistira
Wayang-Golek figure, 19th century
West Java

115 Rama
A Wayang-Kelitik figure, 19th century
East Java

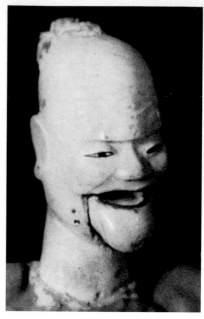

117   A Foolish Old Man
Hand puppet
First half of 19th century
China

116   A Celestial General

Rod puppet, 18th century
China

118   A Servant
Hand puppet
First half of 19th century
China

119   The Emperor Li Si Bin
Hand puppet
First half of 19th century
China

120 and 121   Kiyohime
A trick figure, 1965
Japan

122   Yasha
A Sekkyo-bushi figure
17th century
Japan

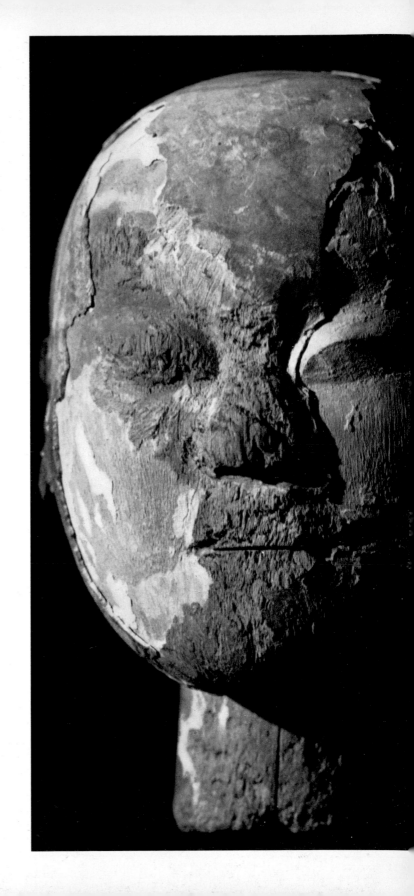

123   Sekkyo-Ningyo
A Sekkyo-bushi figure
17th century
Japan

124 Courtesan
A Bunraku figure
Second half of 19th century
Japan

125 Coptic Priest
Shadow puppet, 14th century
Egypt

126–129 Popular Figures
Beberuhi, Curcunabaz, Zenne, Karagöz
Shadow puppets, 19th century
Turkey

130   Demon (Rakshasa)
Shadow puppet, 19th century
Madras (South India)

132   A Female Dancer
Shadow puppet, 19th century
Madras (South India)

131 Demon (Rakshasa)
Shadow puppet, 19th century
Madras (South India)

133 A Person of Rank
Shadow puppet, 19th century
Madras (South India)

136   Ardjuna
A Wayang-Purwa shadow puppet
Early 20th century
Java

137   Batara Kresna
A Wayang-Purwa puppet
Early 20th century
Java

138   Gunungan
A Wayang-Purwa puppet, 19th century
Bali

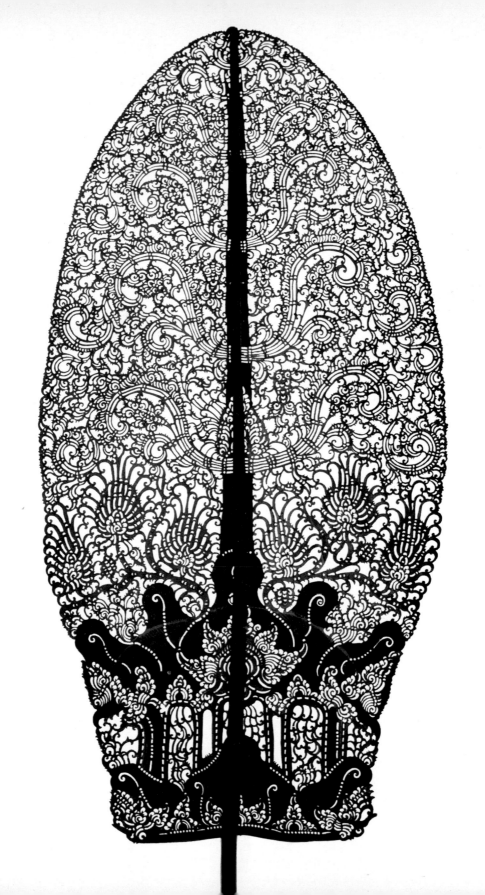

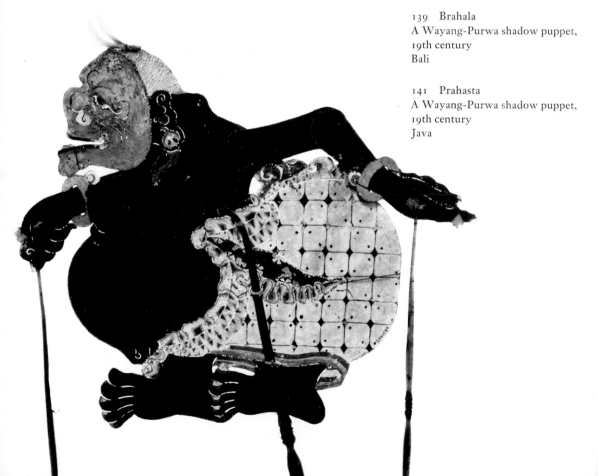

139   Brahala
A Wayang-Purwa shadow puppet,
19th century
Bali

141   Prahasta
A Wayang-Purwa shadow puppet,
19th century
Java

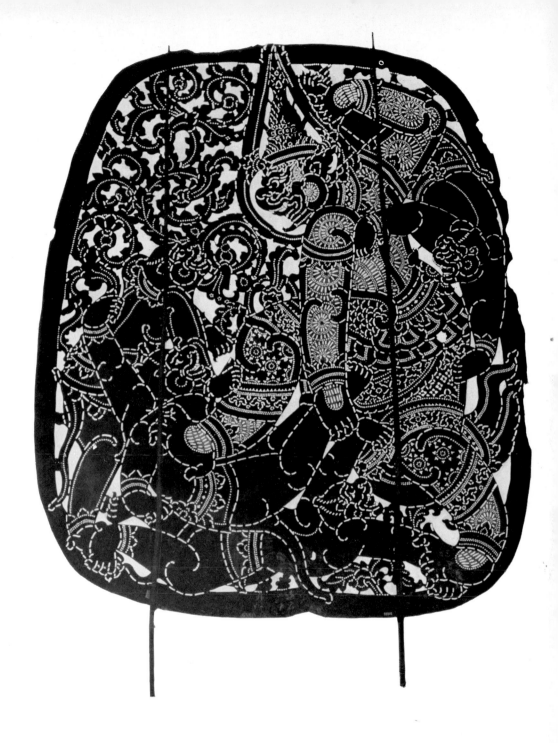

142 Semar
A Wayang-Purwa shadow puppet,
19th century
Java

143 Sukhrip with Four Monkeys
A Nang Luong shadow figure
19th century
Thailand

145 Vishnu
A Nang shadow figure, 19th century
Cambodia

146 Monkey and Guinea fowl
A Nang shadow figure, 19th century
Cambodia

147   Kumphakan
A Nang Luong shadow figure,
19th century
Thailand

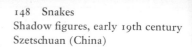

148 Snakes
Shadow figures, early 19th century
Szetschuan (China)

149 Scorpion
Shadow figure, early 19th century
Szetschuan (China)

150 Tortoise
Shadow figure, early 19th century
Szetschuan (China)

151 Cloud
Shadow figure, early 19th century
Szetschuan (China)

152   White Snake and Brother-in-law
Shadow figures, early 19th century
Szetschuan (China)

Next page:

155   House
Shadow figure, early 19th century
Peking

Index

153

154